Contemporary issues
in lifelong learning

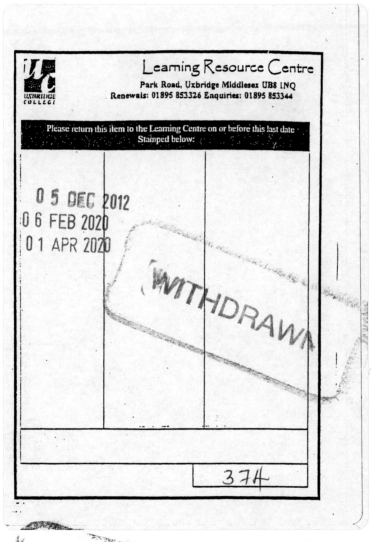

Contemporary issues in lifelong learning

Vicky Duckworth
and
Jonathan Tummons

Mc Graw Hill   Open University Press

Open University Press
McGraw-Hill Education
McGraw-Hill House
Shoppenhangers Road
Maidenhead
Berkshire
England
SL6 2QL

email: enquiries@openup.co.uk
world wide web: www.openup.co.uk

and

Two Penn Plaza, New York, NY 10121-2289, USA

First published 2010

A catalogue record of this book is available from the British Library

ISBN10: 0-33-524112-3 (pb) 0-33-524111-5 (hb)
ISBN13: 978-0-33-524112-5 (pb) 978-0-33-524111-8 (hb)

Library of Congress Cataloging-in-Publication Data
CIP data has been applied for

Typeset by Aptara Inc., India
Printed in the UK by Bell and Bain Ltd, Glasgow.

Fictitous names of companies, products, people, characters and/or data that
may be used herein (in case studies or in examples) are not intended to
represent any real individual, company, product or event.

Mixed Sources
Product group from well-managed
forests and other controlled sources
www.fsc.org   Cert no. TT-COC-002769
© 1996 Forest Stewardship Council

The McGraw·Hill Companies

Vicky: to Anna and Niamh and, as always, Craig Ludlow.

Jonathan: to Jo, Alex and Ellie. And to my parents, Faith and Peter.

Contents

Acknowledgements

Vicky: I would like to thank my students who have been an inspiration in many ways, particularly Catherine Shiel, Danielle Vipond, Lorraine Compton and Angela Lourt-Jackson for contributing case studies to this book. Thanks to my colleagues and particularly to Dr. Ray Dwerryhouse and Matt Cochrane. A very special thanks to Michelle Stephens, Paula Bithells, Sandra Robinson, Sharon Fitzpatrick, Anne Duckworth, Marie McNamara, Jo Meredith and Marie Ludlow for being there and offering insights over a glass of wine.

Jonathan: I would like to thank both my current students at Teesside, and past students at Leeds, Thomas Danby, York College and Yorkshire Coast College. Thanks also to colleagues and friends: John Aston, Suzanne Blake, Jane Brooke, Eleanor Glynn, Roy Fisher, Nick Haigh, Ewan Ingleby, Dawn Joyce, Gaynor Mount, Sharon Powell and Nena Skrbic.

Vicky and Jonathan: thanks to both Stephanie Frosch and Fiona Richman at Open University Press for their constructive advice and endless patience. And special thanks to Mary Hamilton for several years' worth of support, advice, friendship and cups of tea.

Introduction

When we took our first steps as teachers (which is longer ago now than either of us would care to admit), what might be termed the 'professional landscape of the further and adult education sectors' looked very different than it is today. By this we do not mean to say that teachers and trainers used to be 'less professional' than they are now. But the nature of that professionalism has changed. Since the publication of the first professional standards for further education (FE) teachers (the Further Education National Training Organisation (FENTO) standards appeared over 10 years ago now), a variety of structures and organizations have grown up that all have a significant impact on the daily working lives of teachers in the sector. Professional qualifications are now mandatory, and are significantly more rigorous and academically demanding than their counterparts from 10 or more years ago: if you have the time, compare the syllabus for the CertEd/PGCE or DTLLS course that you are on or have recently done with the syllabus for the old City and Guilds 7307 further and adult education teachers' certificate (there are a few to be found on the World Wide Web). The relatively soft touch of an inspection from the Adult Learning Inspectorate has gone, and Ofsted inspections are now a common feature of life in colleges and adult education centres, as well as in schools. A professional body, the Institute for Learning, has been established for all practitioners in the post-compulsory sector, and has responsibility for new Continuing Professional Development (CPD) systems that affect all staff working in the sector.

In fact, being a teacher in further or adult education has changed. Further education colleges, always richly diverse, are now busier than ever, as a result of significant growth in 14–16 and higher education (HE) in FE provision changing the nature of the student population. Adult education classes, so long a refuge from managerial excess and needless paperwork, have now seen the introduction of the Recording and Recognition of Progress and Achievement (RARPA), an assessment tool of debatable validity and reliability, but one that satisfies the requirements of funding bodies. Recreational classes have been all but lost, despite the work of organizations such as CALL (Campaigning Alliance for Lifelong Learning), as the emphasis of successive governments of all hues has moved entirely towards a model of provision that sees education as being solely about economic productivity, rather than about enriching the lives and societies around us.

One of the problems with working in a culture such as this is that it leaves little room to think and breathe. The working lives of teachers in FE colleges in particular are so busy, with so little time to pause, that broader issues such as these are rarely aired, and this is something that needs addressing: hence, this book.

There are a lot of books out there about teaching and learning in the lifelong learning sector (LLS): far more than when we did our 7307s, for example (assuming that anyone did actually read anything; Reece and Walker and Minton were always the two books that tutors referred their students to: these two are still with us, and the former in particular is much better for having gone through extensive revisions). In many ways, the kinds of subject covered by textbooks have not much changed over time. What has changed is the depth and criticality of the coverage. But at a time when FE tutors are busier than ever, and trying to find time and space to read and prepare for their CertEd/PGCE assignments is harder than ever (remembering that the overwhelming majority, some 90 per cent, of teacher-training students in this sector are in-service), making space for the broader issues mentioned above is far from easy. But make room for them we must. Yes, we agree that the Qualified Teacher Learning and Skills (QTLS) framework is important and that professional standards are a good thing, but they can have the effect of closing off areas of discussion and debate. The cry of 'is this going to be in the assessment?', which is so often bemoaned by FE teachers when discussing their students' own instrumental, narrow approach to an overassessed curriculum, is equally heard by teacher educators in colleges and universities.

We have approached the writing of this book from the point of view that wider debates about employability, or inclusivity, or the impact of research, are as immediate and important to the work of a teacher or trainer as are discussions about assessment validity, or learning theories, or motivation. Maybe they should be more important: these latter themes are often wildly distorted. When considering learning theories, it remains a source of puzzlement to us that models such as andragogy (which are so obviously flawed) maintain such a presence in the literature. Or when discussing motivation, the continued references to Maslow are equally puzzling: yes, it is a convenient model, but it fails to address the rich social worlds from which our students come. So in this book we have tried to show how some of these issues (it is a necessarily artificial selection in order to keep the book at a length that we think people have time to read properly) do indeed impact on everyday classroom practice. These are not abstract, overly theoretical, 'out there somewhere' debates: they are concrete, practical and important.

The chapters have been designed to be self-contained, to provide current snapshots of themes that we have encountered in our own teaching practice (we both continue to work with trainee teachers in the sector since taking up university posts, and have many years of experience of working in FE colleges between us) but about which we were unable to recommend a single, well-informed but convenient source of further reading. As such, at one level, the choice of topics covered here has been informed by our students as much as by our own professional judgement and research interests.

How to use this book

This book may be read from cover to cover in one sitting, or it may be read on a chapter-by-chapter basis over a longer period of time. Each chapter is designed so that it can be read in isolation, as and when needed, although references to topics covered in other chapters will be found from time to time.

Within each chapter a number of features can be found that are designed to engage the reader, and to provoke an active response to the ideas and themes that are covered. Objectives at the start of each chapter set the scene, and then the appropriate Lifelong Learning UK (LLUK) professional standards for that chapter are listed. In some places an activity will be found. These activities have been designed to facilitate the practical application of some of the issues covered. The case studies and real-life examples that are to be found in this book are drawn from a variety of different teaching and training contexts, as a reflection of the diversity of the learning and skills sector as a whole. Finally, each chapter finishes with some suggestions for what to do next. A small number of sources, books, journal articles and websites are recommended. These lists are by no means exhaustive: featured items have been chosen because of their suitability and value for use and study by trainee teachers in the learning and skills sector.

1 The changing face of the lifelong learning sector

Chapter objectives

This chapter provides an overview of the sector and explains the changing role of the tutor. To support this it considers Continuing Professional Development (CPD), the Institute for Learning (IfL) and reflective practice. It also considers professionalism, dual professionalism and models of professionalism together with addressing issues of quality and accountability.

The changing role of the tutor

The lifelong learning sector (LLS) teacher workforce is wide and diverse and includes further education (FE) colleges, 6th forms, adult and community learning/personal and community development and learning, offender learning and work-based learning. There are a number of other terms that you may recognize, which include Learning and skills sector (LSS) and the FE sector. FE teachers, sometimes known as FE lecturers, teach students over the age of 16, and some 14–16-year-olds studying work-related subjects.

With the 1992 Further and Higher Education Act came the incorporation of FE colleges and the removal of them from local authority control. This shift brought a greater drive in the direction of a market-led approach with the emphasis on offering appropriate programmes and courses to meet the demands of the market. With the advent of these policies and reforms, the last decade has seen a rapid increase in the number of people attending FE colleges, particularly within the 16–18 age range. This has led to the delivery of subjects in colleges widening and learner cohorts becoming more diverse.

A national framework that Lifelong Learning UK (LLUK) developed to support the development of teachers, from their initial training and development, through to enhancing their continuing personal and professional development profiles (CPD), was implemented across the LLS from September 2007. The shift that took place was a result of governmental legislation that highlighted significant changes to be recognized within what was the sector for post-compulsory education and training (PCET). And the Education Act of 2002 saw the advent of regulations that prohibited anyone from teaching in FE colleges if they had not served a probationary period. The drive was to ensure that learners are only taught by teachers who have received the necessary induction training and who have completed a recognized teaching qualification to cover the essential induction, assessment, monitoring and observation requirements that are considered necessary to teach their specialist subject effectively.

Teachers are, arguably, the most important resource that a student can encounter. Indeed, tutors can influence whether learning is a positive or not so positive experience for the student. Part of the drive to ensure learners have positive experience can be located in the push towards raising the standards of teaching, this is reflected in legislation whereby teachers offered jobs in colleges and other publicly funded organizations are required to have gained an appropriate teaching qualification. This push was supported by the DfES's (2002) *Success for All: Reforming Further Education and Training – Our Vision for the Future* that set out to produce a qualified workforce by 2010. The DfES (2004) *Equipping our Teachers for the Future: Reforming Initial Teacher Training for the Learning and Skills Sector* put forward a policy of reform of teacher development. While the DfES's (2006) White Paper *FE Reform: Raising Skills, Improving Life Chances* introduced further plans for the reprofessionalization of the FE workforce, including CPD for all teachers. The government sees a professional workforce as a key element in realizing its aim to get rid of poor performance in colleges and to enable colleges to respond more effectively to employers' needs. However, the notion of whether equipping teachers with qualifications makes them 'better teachers' is problematic. Questions you may want to consider include:

- Does more qualified mean better motivated?
- Do qualifications offer an indication that the teachers' understanding of the learners' cognitive and emotional needs is better?
- Does being more qualified equate to being more professional?

Some of you may say, yes, that better qualified means a better teacher; and others may argue, no: qualifications do not equate to a better teacher. Whatever your view there is no doubt that being highly competent in both your subject specialist knowledge and pedagogy can lead to best practice in the classroom. As teacher educators we have seen how critical reflection and engagement in key theories can underpin trainees' and qualified teachers' practice. This can empower them to be creative in the classroom and to take innovate approaches that raise the dynamics and promote learner engagement and learning. However, we have also witnessed how qualifications do not always equate to being motivated, driven by the learners' needs, caring, willing to go that extra distance to help learners reach their potential. How can we measure the *emotional capital* (Hochschild, 1983) that many teachers give in their lessons. Most of this is invisible and yet it is the reason why many learners achieve their goals, many in the face of adversity.

Task: role and responsibilities

Consider the role of the professional tutor in the LLS. How might you define the different tasks that tutors are expected to perform?

You may have identified that the role of a professional in the LLS is extremely varied; you may be an assessor, an instructor, a work-based learning or apprentice supervisor, a learning manager, a prison education officer or a community co-ordinator. Most of you will have gained and honed your specialist skill through another trade or profession: for example, as a plumber, lawyer or hairdresser. It is likely that a number of your identities are closely bound in the occupation you have come from rather than in being a practitioner in the sector. Maintaining your professionalism in the sector will include taking responsibility for the education of young people and adults. As a teacher you will work across faculties and disciplines to meet the diverse needs of your learners. In order to do this effectively, communicating effectively is essential; this will include asking questions, seeking advice, and sharing your experiences with other practitioners. One way to support this is through professional networking. Some of you may have already have begun to do this.

In the following case study, Cherry, an art specialist, describes her experiences as a new tutor in an extract taken from her reflective journal.

Case study: the experience of a new tutor

When I first started out as a new teacher I felt isolated. This was probably my fault. What with lesson planning at night and delivering in the day I felt I was on a constant roller coaster. After a while this took its toll on my energy levels and motivations. I even stopped making the space to reflect on my practice. This had an impact on my performance in the classroom. How once I had strived for Best Practice – I began to adopt 'it'll do attitude'. I'm ashamed of this and indeed looking back I now realise I was totally burnt out. It was a colleague who introduced me to a network of practitioners who all shared a similar interest in art. Initially I exchanged emails and then I went to the meetings. It was like a breath of fresh air – we'd all share our stories of teaching – good and bad – and support each other in strategies not only to improve teaching and learning but how to cope with demanding workloads. We also began to get involved in action research. For the first time I was taking ownership of my professional development and it was very empowering. What's more I was working with a group of like minded people who like me were looking for a critical space to support their professional growth. Although I still occasionally feel overwhelmed by the workload, no longer isolated I now feel much more positive knowing I have a support structure of like minded practitioners.

Continuing professional development (CPD)

With an increasing move towards performativity via target setting and results and accountability, many tutors often feel that a great deal of their time and energy is governed
by a managerial-driven system based on close scrutiny of their paperwork rather than
on their practice in the classroom. Avis (2005: 212) identifies how this shift towards
performance management is at odds with the rhetoric of the knowledge economy,
which places an onus on a non-hierarchical approach based on trusting and respectful
relationships between teams. With the managerialist discourse where managers claim
the right to manage and where professional judgements are under intense surveillance,
notions of 'trust' can be something of an illusion. A blame culture can be the result of
such approaches whereby accountability becomes a means by which the institution can
call staff to account. In an age of insecure employment and redundancies, the pressure
to conform to a management agenda can work to erode a practitioner's autonomy and
undermine their professionalism. A way to maintain your professionalism is to keep
up to date with your CPD. You may want to consider how you can take ownership of
this, rather than it being something that is imposed on you. Some common strategies
include:

- getting involved in practitioner research
- becoming a subject specialist coach
- subscribing to a subject specific journal
- attending conferences
- keeping up to date with your reflections
- speaking to your mentor
- planning your CPD for the year so it can be costed into the institution's
  budget
- registering on a CPD module at a college or university.

However, in order to meet the needs of the learners, there does need to be a consideration of the admistration involved that includes assessing their learning styles and
considering learners' motivations and previous experiences. This is a means to identi-
fing various teaching methods that could be utilized meaningfully on the programme
and offers the opportunity to adopt a more personalized approach to teaching and
learning.

Changes to the teacher's role

Rather than the amount of time a tutor spent teaching determining the teaching qualification they took, from September 2007, it shifted to the teaching responsibilities
within the practitioner's role being the driver. So let us consider how the roles differ.

The associate teacher role

The associate teacher role is defined as having fewer teaching responsibilities than the
full role. Importantly, the quality of teaching and learning is expected to be of an equally

high standard. Someone is deemed to be in an associate teacher role if their role and responsibilities are to teach predominantly in at least one of the following ways:

- on a one-to-one basis: for example, tutorial
- from preprepared materials rather than designing the curriculum and materials used
- with a narrow teaching timetable: for example, related to a particular level/ subject/type of learner/short course.

An associate teacher would also be someone whose main occupation is not teaching, but who does deliver learning on a regular or more than occasional basis. This, for example, could be a hairdresser whose main job is hairdressing, but who shares up-to-date skills in the industry. As such an associate tutor will be required to know the learner group. This process will be informed by the initial assessments carried out on learners at the start of their course or programme of study. As an associate teacher a part of your role may include carrying out the initial assessment in your specialist area.

Task

Consider how initial screening and diagnostic results (e.g. in literacy and numeracy) can be used in teaching and learning.

You may have considered:

- course can be set at the right level for the learner
- they can inform an individualized approach
- prepare a lesson that meets the individual needs of learners
- embed literacy, numeracy and information and communication technology (ICT) into the vocational area at the appropriate level
- negotiate individual and meaningful learning goals with learners.

The full teacher role

The role is wider and often comes with more responsibilities. Part of this role will involve using materials and resources that you have designed, implemented and evaluated across a range of levels, subjects and learner types. You may also contribute to other programmes. For example, you may teach law primarily but also input into the business programme.

Task

Consider those aspects of practice that contribute to the full teacher role

---

You may have considered:

- carry out initial assessment with learners
- identify key theories of teaching and learning relevant to your own specialist area
- develop and reflect on practice through reference to relevant theories of learning
- prepare session plans and schemes of work to meet the individual needs of learners
- work as a member of a team; this may be your own specialist team, an inter-agency team, a multidisciplinary team
- work with learners to develop individual learning goals
- develop the curriculum at more than one level to more than one target audience and on more than one programme
- develop teaching and learning materials that are inclusive: e.g. promote readability for learners with dyslexia
- deliver session plans to meet the individual needs of learners, for example, differentiating the aim, objectives and assessment strategies
- provide opportunities for learners to understand how their specialist area relates to a wider social, economic and environmental context, for example, this can be linked to *Every Child Matters*.

You may also have considered:

- monitoring the learners' progress
- keeping accurate records of learner progress; for example, tracking progress in individual learning plans (ILPs)
- contributing to the organizational quality procedures, for example, self-assessment records
- Partake in CPD.

CPD, the IfL and reflective practice

As a trainee teacher or qualified teacher, you can register with the Institute for Learning (IfL). This is a professional body for teachers, trainers, tutors and student teachers in the LLS. Its aim is to support the needs of its members and, importantly, raise the status of teaching practitioners across the sector. The IfL is the body responsible for the regulation of teachers' professional formation. It has a clear set of standards that need to be evidenced in order to achieve a licence to practice. As with other professional bodies, tutors must work within the boundaries of the law and professional values. There are numerous laws and professional ethics that are constantly changing or being updated. Your organization will have its own policies and procedures relating to these legal requirements.

All staff employed as teachers in the LLS must be professionally registered and all new staff must also be licensed to practise by the IfL. As described above, to be licensed, all teachers must be trained to a standard that allows them to achieve either

Qualified Teacher Learning and Skills (QTLS) status or Associate Teacher Learning and Skills (ATLS) status, depending on their role. All full-time teachers, which includes those who are new and existing, should undertake at least 30 hours of CPD per year and keep a record reflecting on the CPD activities they have undertaken to maintain their status with the IfL. Those in part-time employment will undertake CPD on a pro rata basis, with a minimum of six hours a year.

Reflective practice

Learning from experience is one of the aims of critical reflection. It is known as experiential learning. For a number of teachers the best part of teaching is the learning and growth they get from it. This can have a profound impact that challenges and changes your previously held values, beliefs and assumptions.

In order to begin the reflecting, you may want to place the learner at the centre of the cycle and consider:

- Where are my learners coming from: for example, are they school leavers, are they adult returnees, are you working in an economically deprived or an affluent area?
- What do they need to know and how can I help facilitate the access to this knowledge to keep them growing and reaching their potential?
- How can I best support them on their learning journey?
- Do I need to work with other professionals, for example, a counsellor?
- Do I need to signpost them to specialists, for example, a dyslexia specialist?

Part of the excitement and the challenge of being a tutor is getting to know each student. In order to do this you will need to understand how education fits into their lives, for example, what are their goals and aspirations? You may also want to consider how their assumptions, beliefs and values inhibit or enhance their personal/professional growth. Helping learners realize their potential may mean creating an environment where you can both reflect and challenge long-held beliefs in order for you and your learners to move forward.

Models of reflection

The importance of reflecting on what you are doing, as part of the learning process, has been explored by a number of people. David Kolb (1984) asserts that knowledge results from the interaction between theory and experience. He states that learning takes place in four stages in a cycle that continues the more one learns (see Fig. 1.1).

According to Kolb, learning is the process whereby knowledge is created through the transformation of experience. It is worth thinking of his model as you analyse, reflect and write about your practice. This will help you to demonstrate where and how you have created knowledge through the experiences you have gone through. You may

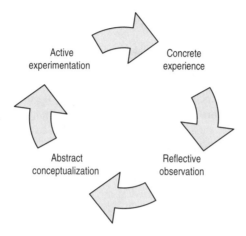

Source: Kolb (1984)

Figure 1.1 The four stages of the adult learning process

want to share your experiences and the cycle these take with your mentor, specialist subject coach or manager. Following the Kolb model can be the basis for a meaningful dialogue on:

- discussion of concrete experience
- analysis of experience
- conceptual learning
- application of learning
- additionally, you will be rated in areas of documentation and writing skills.

By using Kolb's model, you can reflect on past learning experiences and form a strong structure for future learning. This will be vital in continuing to gain their licence to practise and future CPD.

In this extract from her reflective journal, Catherine explores her recent experience of being observed in her teaching practice, drawing on Kolb's experiential learning model to aid her writing.

Case study: reflecting on experience

Yesterday I completed my first observed lesson, observed by my mentor and tutor. It was also the first time I had taught a class on my own, as previous experiences have involved observations and team teaches.

The class I was taking is considered a difficult cohort with some students requesting a transfer to another class. It is a diverse cohort with diverse needs. Due to the labelling of my cohort (which I don't agree with) I had spent time observing learners in class and reviewing Individual Learning Plans to develop my own conclusions. I also discussed with fellow teachers.

I had planned and prepared well for the session. I was pleased with my preparation and organisation and benefited from making reference back to a key handout provided and an exercise completed in one of our sessions. I think at this early stage in my learning journey, such documents are extremely useful resources and tools to lean on until I begin to develop my own way of doing things. In some ways I found the planning process a challenge as there are many levels on which you are planning. For example, I was planning for my observation and wanted to tick X amount of boxes for that. I was also planning for my cohort and wanted to tick certain boxes for them as individuals and then there is the curriculum, I had certain boxes to tick for that. It did beg the question who/what am I really planning for? Does it all lead to the same thing? And if not, there are professional challenges to that. As such I am looking forward to the next semester when we will explore this debate in more detail.

Having researched behaviour and classroom management theories I felt confident and having observed right and wrong approaches during previous observations I felt confident in managing the class. For example when Alexandras came in late I paused while he sat down and used a stare that prompted an apology. I felt on the whole the group were engaged and really made an effort to participate. I felt respected and trusted and feel confident the rapport will continue to grow my cohort.

Using positive reinforcement and feedback strategies really worked and the class really responded to specific comments I made about 'when they get a job/go to university'. How mature their questions were and how well they completed the numeracy exercise! It felt really satisfying to see them smile proudly to themselves.

I did find quieter learners more difficult to bring in. And knowing their personal circumstances I didn't want to pick on them by name, but at the same time knew I should have done more to bring them in more. It makes me feel like I've failed. But at the end of the day I need to find the balance that is right for them, not what makes me feel good. This is something to work on.

In my rationale, my teaching and learning strategies were varied to reach all learners needs and allow for scaffolding. However, on reflection I let myself down by relying on myself being able to pose questions and assess understanding across different levels off my own back. I think because I did this in my previous role so well I set myself a trap. In my old role I was working with a different level and was an expert deliverer at that level. I found it challenging to come up with suitable links and examples for my learners during the session and it affected my confidence. I realised immediately that in future I need to plan for questioning, pre-prepare questions at a higher and lower order where possible to help me develop my practice until I become more experienced at it. I definitely feel that questioning skills are crucial to be effective in class assessment and something that is learned and practised to achieve skill and will endeavour to do this.

I was disappointed with the Grade 3 grade. On reflection, I think it is because I don't like the term 'satisfactory' and it is too near to a Grade 4. So I'm getting hung up on numbers and words. (Another debate for assessment!) However, ultimately it is the quality of the feedback, experience and my learning from it that matters and considering this was my first solo teach and first observation to start at a 3 is a reasonable starting point. I do feel that there were some elements that would have scored a 2 and so I need to focus on moving those elements at a 3 up to a 2 also.

In summary I would have definitely sought out more examples to bring to the learners' level. The response to the Who am I? Exercise was evidence that speaking their language really engaged the learners and the buzz in the room during that exercise is what I want to create. I also need to develop my skills in questioning to improve my assessment in class. On one level I know everyone has completed exercises, answered questions etc. But I want to be able to apply strategies that let me know understanding is there and can be applied otherwise the learning will be lost. Connecting my teaching, learning and assessment strategies together will definitely help me to achieve more success (see Table 1.1).

Table 1.1 Action plan

Action	How	By when	How will it I know I've achieved it?
Develop my questioning skills	Research theories and look for ways to apply them in the next lesson. Build in a questioning assessment strategy for my next lesson	Next observed session TBC	Stronger questioning skills More confident delivery More learner responses Greater validity and reliability of assessment of learning that has taken place
Demonstrate clearer links between learning objectives, teaching and assessment strategies	Develop a mind-map approach to planning a lesson that can be used ongoing	Ongoing	More clarity to see what was planned, delivered and how it was assessed. Improved reliability of assessment
Develop wider examples and experiences for subject content	For each topic I introduce I will prepare an example in advance, whether from own experience or specifically chosen to appeal to learners' experiences	Next observed session TBC	Resource file started which includes stored examples and experiences that can be shared and stored for future use

Other perspectives: Gibbs' reflective cycle

Gibbs (2007) identified a series of six steps to aid reflective practice; these elements make up a cycle that can be applied over and over.

- Description – what happened?
- Feelings – what were you thinking and feeling?
- Evaluation – what was good and bad about the experience?
- Analysis – what sense can you make of the situation?
- Conclusion – what else could you have done?
- Action plan – what will you do next time?

In this session, Catherine shares her reflection following the Gibb model.

Case study: reflecting on a difficult session

I had planned well and had prepared a variety of resources and activities. The class I was taking is considered a difficult cohort and I have managed to maintain a good learning environment with them in previous sessions. Despite this I was apprehensive about how it would go. Earlier in the day I was made aware that this group were behind on their assignments and their behaviour was noted across a number of classes as being challenging.

I was concerned that no matter how good the resources and content may have been, if their minds are elsewhere then learning will not take place. I reflected on how I would deliver the session and considered running a revision session. I was advised by my mentor and the course leader to continue as planned. I tried hard to show them how the content would help them complete their assignment and give it value and went in with the belief that if I delivered a good session it would 'snap them out of it'.

That didn't happen, at every opportunity a group of girls persisted with complaints and questions regarding assignment work. They refused to engage in the session. This interrupted the session flow and disengaged those who were ready to learn and had completed the assignment already.

But the session was exhausting, and did not feel like a good session at all. Certainly one I wouldn't want to repeat. My mentor came in half way through and he agreed 'not a great session'.

We acknowledged the difficult cohort and the challenges that were outside of my control. Rather than dwell on those we discussed how I could handle the situation better next time round. I could, for example, agree to finish the session early to review the assignment again, next time I will take time at the beginning of the session to do this to get rid of as much baggage as possible before the session starts and then agree steps forward that will settle learners and allow us to continue. I also allowed the staffroom comments and advice to affect my own judgement.

In delivering the session I felt I overcompensated in trying to show learners the value of the content. This resulted in me directing a lot of information and resources at the learners, rather than engaging them and the session needed to be more student-led and I should have focused my time and energy on getting them involved.

I agreed with my mentor that these learners do need to take more responsibility for their learning, and expressed my belief that with future assignments we need to build in strategies to support them do this as they are really struggling. Race and Pickford's (2007: 6) Ten-point Plan for retaining your students includes Point 3, 'Build in Study Skills Guidance in to Your Sessions as "Many argue that short, localised bursts of study skills advice have more impact than larger, generic study skills sessions"'.

At the end of the session I asked for feedback from my learners as to the value of the session. My mentor was surprised by this and he acknowledged my 'bravery' as it could have been negative under the circumstances.

We were both genuinely surprised with the feedback on the learning that was achieved. It highlighted to me how important it is to include assessment and feedback strategies, even when you may fear the results will not be as you hoped. Had I not done what I did at the end of the session I would have assumed it was a complete disaster.

In future I will respond to learner anxieties before commencing a lesson. I will plan some 'plan B' activities in readiness. I also need to recognise my own response and my tendency to 'do all the work in difficult situations, and facilitate more student-centred activities'. Not only will this benefit and engage learners more, it will be less exhausting for me too.

What initially felt like the session from hell, on reflection has become one of real learning and development for me. I feel more confident to manage this situation again. I have seen the value in feedback and assessment in the hardest of sessions and have challenged my own practice more than in previous sessions. I guess it really is a case of what doesn't break you only makes you stronger.

It is important to add that this reflection was only realised after several days of reflecting on the session. If I wrote this the same day or even the following day, my experience would be a different one. Petty's (200: 319) advises caution on coming to any fixed conclusions straight away and suggests making some immediate notes, as you will probably 'think more clearly after you have "slept on in it".' That appears to be the case for me (see Table 1.2).

Writing reflections can vary

A way to reflect is to keep a diary of your thoughts, feelings and experiences. The chances are you will be writing them down in a number of places. This will often depend on

Table 1.2 Action plan

Action	How	By when	How will I know I've achieved it?
Collate a series of revision activities to address assignment concerns	Speak to mentor and peers for suggestions and existing resources Research web/further reading	End of February	Collection of activities ready to use Assessment of activity when used
Research study skills activities to build into sessions	Speak to mentor and peers for suggestions and existing resources Research web/further reading	March	Included in assignment I am designing for BND Unit 4 Students demonstrate improved knowledge of assignment and what is expected

where you are and what is the most accessible. For example, you may make notes after a lesson and then word-process them later.

They may be written in:

- learning journals, a diary and so on
- reflection on work experiences
- reflection on placement experiences, for example, communication with a mentor, subject specialist coach or manager
- lesson evaluations
- professional development portfolio.

Reflections are not just for when you are trainee teacher, they are something you will need to produce throughout your career. Indeed, it is an integral part of your CPD. It can offer you a deeper understanding of a number of areas in both your personal and public life.

Tips for good reflection

- Keep a journal with you so you can note your reflections at any time. It is surprising how ideas can pop up when least expected!
- Remember, you do not have to show anyone your reflections, so be honest. If you need to, ask your tutor or mentor for input.
- Listen to the voice of your learners, include their ideas and feelings in your reflections.
- Do not be too hard on yourself. Celebrate what you can do as well as what you would like to develop.
- Reflections do not need to be in word form, you may want to draw your reflections, take photographs and so on. Find a medium that allows you to express yourself and your feelings.

Dual professionalism

The distinctive model of initial teacher training for LLS recognizes that teachers and trainers are recruited for their vocational and subject skills and knowledge and that they bring to the sector substantial expertise from their background, in business, industry, commerce or careers in the public or voluntary sectors. Indeed, for the majority of teachers and trainers, teaching in LLS is a second or third career. As such they are often professionals in their own field before they start their teaching career. For example, you could be a nurse working in a hospital or perhaps a bricklayer working in construction, before considering teaching your subject. There are two components of your professionalism: your subject specialism and the pedagogy related to that area. This is what is referred to as 'dual professionalism' and both are equally important in your role as a tutor or trainer. It is therefore essential that both these area are considered when you address your CPD.

Quality assurance and administration

As a teacher in the LLS, you have a responsibility to ensure that you behave in an appropriate way. To ensure a unified expectation of behaviour and conduct across the sector, the IfL developed a 'Code of Professional Practice', which all its members need to adhere to. A responsibility of the trainee and qualified teacher is to continually reflect and move towards best practice. As your understanding of the sector and your learners changes so will your needs. This will be reflected in continual reassessment. A way to move forward is to evaluate and improve the quality and impact of your practice and in doing so take into account your learners' changing needs. Part of your role will also be keeping up-to-date and accurate records; failure to so can be classed as gross misconduct in some organizations. The array of paperwork encountered by tutors can be bewildering:

- Health and Safety – risk assessments, accident reports, fire evacuation procedures and so on.
- Teaching records – attendance registers, syllabuses, schemes of work, session plans, assessments, including initial assessments (ILPs).
- Auditing and accountability – enrolment forms, learner satisfaction questionnaires (evaluation forms), data-gathering for funding bodies (attendance/completion/achievement stats/progression routes).

Conclusion

The drive in the learning and skills sector is to upskill the sector's workforce and turn what was (and many think still is) the Cinderella profession into the profession of *choice*. However, there remain issues of contention. Teachers in FE, including those who gain

QTLS professional status for teaching in FE and skills sector, are not able to teach in a school's context unless they are qualified schoolteachers. Schoolteachers, on the other hand, are allowed to teach in FE settings, because Qualified Teacher Status (QTS) is recognized as meeting the qualification threshold. With their distinctive and up-to-date vocational expertise, and their ability to contribute more fully to the 14–19 curriculum, tutors in the LLS play an increasingly important role in the delivery of vocational qualifications. Yet parity of pay and conditions with schoolteachers continues to elude them. This clearly needs to be addressed if the LLS is to become the career of choice and vocational skills are to be valued as much in reality as the rhetorics of politicians.

References

Avis, J. (2005) Beyond performativity: reflections on activist professionalism and the labour process in further education, *Journal of Education Policy*, 202: 209–22.

Department for Education and Skills (DfES) (2002) *Success for All: Reforming Futher Education and Training – Our Vision for the Future*. Available online at www.dfes.gov.uk

Department for Education and Skills (DfES) (2004) *Equipping our Teachers for the Future: Reforming Initial Training for the Learning and Skills Sector*. Available online at www.dfes.gov.uk

Department for Education and Skills (DfES) (2006) *FE Reform: Raising Skills, Improving Life Chances*. Available online at www.dfes.gov.uk

Gibbs, S. (2007) *Human Resources Development: Processes, Practices and Perspectives*. London: Prentice Hall.

Hochschild, A. (1983) *The Managed Heart: Commercialization of Human Feeling*. Berkeley, CA: University of California Press.

Kolb, D.A. (1984) *Experiential Learning: Experience as the Source of Learning and Development*. Upper Saddle Row: Prentice Hall.

Race, P. and Pickford, R. (2007) *Making Teaching Work: 'Teaching Smarter' in Post Compulsory Education*. London: Sage Publications.

2 Widening participation and inclusive practice

Chapter objectives

This chapter offers an overview of how and why key aspects of educational provision have changed in Britain in order to widen access to education. To begin with, it looks at definitions of widening participation and explores the *Every Child Matters* framework. It also examines the impact of the widening participation agenda on curriculum development and considers educational provision in multidisciplinary and inter-agency teams. Finally, this chapter considers teaching roles in wider professional settings, which include working in homeless shelters, family learning provision and working with offenders.

Professional standards

This chapter addresses the following professional practice standards for Qualified Teacher Learning and Skills (QTLS):

AK 3.1 **Issues of equality, diversity and inclusion.**

AK 5.1 **Ways to communicate and collaborate with colleagues and/ or others to enhance learner's experience.**

BK 1.1 **Ways to maintain a learning environment in which learners feel safe and supported.**

FK 1.1 **Sources of information, advice, guidance and support to which the learners might be referred.**

FK 4.2 **Processes for liaison with colleagues and other professionals to provide effective guidance and support for learners.**

(LLUK, 2006)

Introduction

Changes in the UK economy over the last 50 years have been accompanied by changing patterns of employment that are increasingly experienced as insecure and transient. In what is sometimes called the post-industrial society, it would seem to be the case that there are no longer 'jobs for life' that, following an initial period of training (whether this be a degree or an apprenticeship), we might expect to remain in for the majority of our working lives. Instead, we have to be lifelong learners, willing to engage in further training as and when required to maintain job security. So, if more people have to be learners for longer periods of adult life, it follows that appropriate opportunities for learning need to be provided. At the same time, if the UK economy is going to be able to compete in a global marketplace (whatever one of those might be), then the UK workforce as a whole is going to need to be qualified at ever-higher levels.

The need to constantly upskill the UK workforce is not, however, the only reason why more people need to be encouraged to take part in education and training. Widening access to education is also seen as being beneficial to society in a wider sense to help combat social exclusion. In this context, current debates about lifelong learning retain some aspect of what was once known as 'the liberal tradition of adult learning': the sense that access to learning for adults was a social and cultural benefit in itself. Consequently, in order to support the UK economy, combat social exclusion and engender social justice, educational provision needs to be made available to anyone and everyone who might benefit from it.

But it is important to remember that these are not the only ways in which widening participation might currently be understood. The provision of 'learning for pleasure' or 'recreational' classes continues to make up a significant component of Local Educational Authority (LEA) educational programmes. Organizations such as the Workers' Educational Association (WEA) and the University of the Third Age (U3A) also continue to provide courses of study in languages, local and family history, or philosophy for beginners.

'Widening participation' came to mean something quite specific during the lifetime of the previous, Labour, Government. This is not to belie the importance of earlier programmes and initiatives designed to encourage more people to take part in educational provision of one kind or another. The so-called 'new universities' of the 1960s (such as Bristol, Lancaster, Sussex, Warwick and York) are a good example. Now numbered among the more prestigious research-led universities in the UK, they can be seen as being originally built in order to widen provision in higher education (HE) at a time when only a very small number of people went to university.

Widening participation

Current discourses about widening participation can be dated back particularly to the publication of the Dearing Report (HEFCE, 1997a) and Kennedy Report (HEFCE, 1997b). It has been used and applied in many aspects of education and for many is a 'buzzword', which is defined in terms of particular groups that are under-represented within a particular kind of institution (e.g. further education (FE)) or within a curriculum area (e.g. Information Communication Technology (ICT)). It has also been widely discussed in relation to access to HE. Social class differentials in HE participation rates have been the key to understanding under-representation and to taking steps to widen participation in HE (Thomas, 2001; Reay et al., 2005). Gender, ethnicity and disability are other factors that are addressed.

The terms 'widening participation', 'inclusive practice' and 'differentiation' are often used both simultaneously and interchangeably within the lifelong learning sector (LLS). The concepts support each other in offering inclusive approaches to meet the increasingly diverse needs of learner populations, although each term does have a particular focus.

Widening participation is the process by which colleges, universities and other providers (such as local education authorities, charitable institutions and voluntary organizations) take steps to recruit and then support learners who, due to their social, economic or ethnic backgrounds, or other personal or environmental factors, are less likely to take part in education and training or are seen as being at risk from social exclusion.

Inclusive practice is an approach to teaching and learning that endeavours to encourage the fullest participation of learners and that recognizes and respects equality and diversity. An inclusive approach, in its widest sense, encompasses not only the widening participation agenda, or the need for differentiation, but also provision for students with seen or unseen disabilities or other learning difficulties.

Differentiation is the approach to teaching and learning that both recognizes the individuality of learners and also informs ways of planning for learning and teaching that take these individualities into consideration. A differentiated approach may be relatively informal (i.e. a tutor may decide to use different activities with different learners in order to achieve the same goals) or more formal (such as having different learners within the same group following different syllabuses).

Task: exploring mission statements

Institutions' mission statements frequently reflect the widening participation agenda. This is hardly surprising, as it is the source of considerable political – and financial – focus. Read the example of the short mission statement below. Identify how it reflects an ethos of widening participation:

> *The college's values are the development of a fully integrated learning community based around the programmes they are on in which students are treated according to their need, with parity of esteem irrespective of their background, race, gender, age, ambition, previous education and subject or level of study.*

Now look at the mission statement at the college where you work, or where you are on a teaching placement, and consider how it addresses these issues.

Meeting the needs of learners

Widening participation however is about far more than recruiting a wider range of school-leavers. It involves thinking about mature, part-time and work-based students. It is about considering the participation of learners on their learning journey throughout the life course. For many students, the LLS offers a second or even final chance to obtain the qualifications and skills that they need to move forward in their life. This might involve gaining a qualification that is needed to find employment, to change employment, or to return to the workplace after time spent looking after elderly relatives or starting a family. Colleges and other providers are therefore pivotal in terms of both social integration and the opportunities for professional and personal development that they offer. The LLS also plays an important role in accommodating those learners who, for reasons to do with their social or economic backgrounds, might otherwise not engage in education or training. Indeed, unless providers in the LLS address the social issues that often impact on learners' entry behaviour (such as lack of finance, or lack of family support), then the ability of their learners to succeed may be undermined. Learners need to feel valued, confident and safe so that they can engage effectively.

Discussion about the barriers the learners face can play a vital role in providing supportive responses to them. Programmes need to offer a wide range of accessible supports. Using holistic approaches that help learners feel valued and respected, and signposting them to supportive and informative agencies and networks are therefore vital. Barriers to learning can be practical, even prosaic: whether or not a student can access public transport might, for example, prevent them from attending a course. Funding is frequently cited as a cause for concern, and the ways in which financial support can be obtained are not always transparent. More specific personal or emotional issues can be managed through the intervention of support workers or student counsellors. Students with specific learning difficulties can receive help from learning support workers such as note-takers or British sign language (BSL) interpreters, and can apply for funding to buy assistive technologies.

So, if we accept that widening participation somehow refers to those policy drivers that help organizations to recruit and retain ever-wider and more diverse groups of students, we need to consider how what we do as teachers and trainers helps such students to make the most of their opportunities to participate in learning. In all aspects of our practice, we need to be mindful of different needs, the impact that outside factors can have on classroom behaviours, and the histories and biographies of our learners. To put it another way, we need all aspects of our practice to be inclusive.

From widening participation to inclusive practice

'Inclusive practice' is an expression that occurs frequently in policy documents, textbooks such as this one, and leaflets and bulletins from the Learning and Skills Improvement Service (LSIS) or one of its predecessor organizations. College staff development managers hold training days on inclusive practice. New members of teaching staff in the LLS have to go to induction events where they learn about it. It is a key component of the teacher-training syllabus for the LLS. But it does not appear anywhere in the Lifelong Learning UK (LLUK) professional standards framework, where the broader term 'inclusion' is used instead, nor does it appear in the Institute for Learning's (IfL) Code of Professional Practice. Its meaning is quite broad and in some ways hard to pin down; this is perhaps a reflection of the many ideas or concepts that are running in the background when, as practitioners, we discuss inclusive practice.

From the outset, let us state what an inclusive approach does *not* entail. Inclusive practice is not, or should not, be somehow conflated with a sense of automatic, universal entitlement, an uncritical acceptance of everybody's right to access a particular kind of education or training provision, or a particular course or programme of study, with no concern for any sort of mitigating factors. Admissions guidelines, pre-entry tests and course criteria are important aspects of curriculum design and help to ensure that learners are not set up to fail by being allowed to study on a programme or course that is either unsuited to them or which they are unsuited to. Nonetheless they can be deviated from if appropriate professional judgements are taken into account. A good example of this is the debate as to whether or not the 'A' level grades of students from socially deprived areas should be given the same value as those of students from affluent areas when applying to universities. Unfortunately, such guidelines are sometimes ignored for reasons of expediency. It is not uncommon for managers in colleges or adult education centres to put pressure on admissions tutors to find a place for a particular student or group of students on a course that they are not qualified to be on. Usually such actions are driven by funding: the need to ensure a certain number of enrolments so that a particular admissions or funding target can be met.

So what is inclusive practice? We would suggest that it is best thought of as a way of approaching teaching and learning (in both a theoretical and a practical sense) so that what we do, in the broadest sense, is available to the widest possible potential student audience, as long as we are confident that they are being given the right advice about how they should be mapping out their learning journeys. By 'right advice', we do not mean to reduce participation, to turn learners away just because a course or programme that they wish to study may not, for example, lead to eventual employment in that vocational or technical area. But once enrolled on a programme, we need to be as confident as we can be that there are no barriers – institutional, pedagogical or practical – that would unfairly impact on some students.

Inclusive practice, therefore, is a concern for not only tutors, but college managers and leaders as well. It is not just a matter of performing particular technical tasks that might, for example, allow a student with a physical disability to enrol on an Access to HE course. It is a state of mind, a professional value, almost an ethical consideration. An inclusive learning environment does not begin and end at the door to a classroom or workshop: a well-designed college classroom that provides easy access for learners who are wheelchair users is of little use if the college learning resource centre is so designed that too many of the books kept there are physically out of their reach. The modification of summative assessment methods to take account of specific learner needs (such as allowing a support worker for learners with dyslexia, or the use of assistive computer equipment) is of little use if the learner in question has not already received support throughout their programme of study. Inclusive practice needs to become part of the repertoire of anyone working in the LLS. The reality, however, is that it is invariably the tutor who acts as the first point of contact for those learners who need assistance, or have questions about the support that they might be entitled to receive.

From inclusive practice to differentiation

If inclusive practice is taken to be a broad ethical or professional set of values, then differentiation takes us into the workshop or classroom. When we discuss a differentiated approach to learning and teaching, we are talking about those practical steps, the ways in which we plan and prepare our activities or assessments that allow a more or less diverse group of students to participate and, hence, to learn. There are two main ways in which we can consider differentiation in our lesson planning:

1 Differentiation by outcome
  When differentiating by outcome, tutors set different learning outcomes in the knowledge that they will apply to different students within the group. A common approach is to consider wording outcomes so that they indicate which outcomes all students will meet, and which outcomes only some will meet. It is common for the institutional lesson plan templates that are used by FE colleges and adult education providers to include boxes for both universal and partial differentiated outcomes, as well as a box labelled 'differentiation', or similar, where the tutor can make any additional notes regarding the outcomes and activities that they are planning.
2 Differentiation by activity (including assessment)
  In some cases, students will work to different outcomes. In other cases, students will work to the same outcomes, but will engage in different kinds of activity or assessment in order to achieve them. Therefore, tutors plan a variety of activities that will help learners work towards the outcomes in a number of different ways. Tasks may be chosen according to their suitability to the topic at hand, or according to the learning styles of the students. However, learning styles are controversial and lack reliability, and although they are popular with managers and staff development officers (because they are an easy and convenient way of evidencing differentiation), they should not be used in isolation when planning activities and assessments.

However, these approaches all assume that the students are working towards the same qualification or within the same programme of study. It is not uncommon for tutors to find themselves teaching mixed groups: by this, we mean a group of students who are working towards different qualifications, but who share a classroom or workshop, facilities and a tutor, all at the same time.

Case studies: mixed classrooms

As you read through the following case studies (which are authentic), consider what the advantages or disadvantages to running such mixed sessions might be.

Case study 1: adult basic education

Shazia is an adult education lecturer who works in a large city in Northern England, teaching English as a second language to a very diverse group of students. The local authority employs her on an hourly basis. Some have lived in England for a long time and are quite capable of conversing in English, but need to gain a formal qualification in order to secure employment. Others have only recently arrived, and some are refugees. There are only eleven students in the class. Some are working towards a level one qualification, some are working towards entry level one and others are working towards entry level two. Shazia has to juggle three different syllabuses and three different sets of summative assessment requirements. And she is required to write three different lesson plans for each two-hour meeting, one for each syllabus.

Case study 2: beauty therapy

Julie is a full-time lecturer working in a busy further education college. She has taught beauty therapy for three years, after several years working in the industry. On Thursdays, she teaches underpinning theory sessions to a mixed group: some of the girls (the students are all girls) are working towards a level two NVQ; the others are working towards a level three NVQ.

Case study: conclusions

The practicalities behind such an approach are relatively straightforward. It must surely be preferable to have a mixed class rather than no classes at all. And both Shazia and Julie are for the most part happy with the progress that the students are making in the classroom. Certainly, the students in question do not seem to be unduly worried. But the amount of preparation and paperwork is more of a problem, as Shazia writes:

Case study 1 (cont.): about basic education

In effect, I am teaching three classes at the same time. It's exhausting: I have to move from group to group, get each one started with their next task and then leave the learning support worker to watch things until I can get round to them again. I think the higher level learners are okay, but the entry two ones do not understand everything that is going on, I'm sure of it. But there isn't a separate class to move them to – either they stay with me or that's it. So I have to do all the handouts in different ways, all the assignments – and I even have to do three lesson plans and they won't let me just write one. But I still just get paid three hours, even though it takes me that long just to get the planning done.

Are such mixed classes a good idea? If integrating level two and level three students is so seamless, so straightforward, does this not challenge the very notion of 'levels' of student learning and work? Should mixed-ability teaching be the norm, and streaming be the exception?

Inclusive approaches: curricular and political responses

The Qualifications and Curriculum Authority (QCA) has been a lead player in the reforms for both young people and adults in relation not only to qualifications themselves but also to the whole system within which qualifications are positioned. Over recent years, a number of significant changes have been introduced:

- the 14–19 Diplomas
- raising the age at which young people have to be either in school or college, or receiving other formal education or training
- the reform of vocational qualifications
- the introduction of functional skills and the move away from key skills
- the introduction of the foundation learning tier.

These are all discrete processes, but have all been part of the previous Labour Government's 14–19 Agenda (at the time of writing, an aim at least broadly shared by the new Conservative/Liberal Democrat coalition government); the overall aim of which is to increase an uptake in formal education and training, raise achievement levels (i.e. increase the number of people who attain formal qualifications) and hence raise overall levels of employability and economic activity (although the extent to which a more qualified workforce is automatically more productive, an idea much touted by the current government, is in fact open to serious criticism (Gee et al., 1996).

Over the last few years *Raising Skills, Improving Life Chances* (the Labour Government's FE *White Paper*, DCSF, 2006) has led in policy terms to initiatives both on the supply and demand side. These have included significant structural change in the agencies and bodies responsible for implementing a raft of reforms, which includes the education and employment sector. The *Skills For Growth Strategy in Britain* (BIS, 2009) may be viewed as placing employers centre stage, acknowledging a growing recognition that skills and knowledge are essential in determining the ability of the nation to compete in the global economy. This is also reflected in the earlier government Green Paper *The Learning Age* (LLUK, 1998), which drew on the argument that knowledge and the pursuit of knowledge have become the key factors shaping a globally competitive economy. It spoke of the importance of skills to both individuals and employers and to the nation. It set out a course of actions based on greater employer engagement; more responsive provision and reform of qualifications on the supply side; and raising ambition, motivating and supporting individuals and employers on the demand side. Subsequently 'demand-led' became an expression widely used in education. The curriculum today may be viewed as being 'demand-led' by the needs of the global economy with an emphasis on the notion of competitiveness going hand in hand with a more general ambition of social inclusion, perhaps best personified by *Every Child Matters* (DfES, 2004).

Every Child Matters (ECM)

In 2003 the Labour Government published a *Green Paper* called *Every Child Matters*. This was published alongside the formal response to the report into the death of Victoria Climbié. The Victoria Climbié Inquiry Report (2003) stated that:

> It is deeply disturbing that during the days and months following the initial contact with Ealing Housing Department, Victoria was known to over ten other agencies. On twelve key occasions relevant services had the opportunity to intervene in Victoria's life.

The fundamental tenet of *Every Child Matters* is for government agencies to work more effectively across multidisciplinary and inter-agency teams to protect vulnerable children and adults; an issue that clearly arises from protection of the vulnerable is safeguarding:

> Safeguarding and promoting the welfare of children ... depends on effective joint working between agencies and professionals that have different roles and expertise. Individual children, especially some of the most vulnerable children and those at greatest risk of social exclusion, will need co-ordinated help from health, education, children's social care, and quite possibly the voluntary sector and other agencies.
>
> (HM Government, 2006)

Every Child Matters: Change for Children (DfES, 2004), which covers children from birth–19, was passed into law by the Children Act of 2004, and consists of the following five points that are defined as being necessary for the growth and development of children and young adults:

1   Being healthy
2   Staying safe
3   Enjoying and achieving
4   Making a positive contribution
5   Achieving economic well-being.

Task: putting *ECM* into practice

Look again at the five *ECM* objectives and consider what your place of work or placement provider does to:

- promote the well-being of its learners and staff?
- keep its learners safe and well cared for?
- promote healthy and healthy lifestyles for learners and staff?
- ensure learners enjoy their learning and achieve their optimum potential?
- enable learners to make a positive contribution?
- promote learners to achieve economic well-being?
- respond to learners' emotional, social and behavioural difficulties?

Now consider the extent to which the place you work or have your placement supports staff well enough to enable them to promote and design curricula that address the *ECM* agenda.

Institutional responses to *ECM* in the lifelong learning sector

The following activities are commonly found to support the *ECM* agenda in the lifelong learning sector:

1   Being healthy
     Lunchtime clubs, healthy eating projects, sports and physical activity (e.g. a gym club), activities that promote emotional well-being, drugs awareness and sexual health programmes. These can sometimes be delivered by mentors or invited expert speakers such as nurses, youth workers or counsellors.
2   Staying safe
     Ensuring a safe environment for young and older people during and after college, anti-bullying programmes, peer mentoring or 'buddying' and peer mediation, mentor support, strong tutorial system, first aid, self-defence classes, mediation courses, opening for critical reflection and consciousness raising.
3   Enjoying and achieving
     Activities that extend, enrich and enable, building on curriculum subjects and social practices, hobbies or interests from home, offering extra support, new skills and interests, performing arts, music, opportunities to enjoy and experience success, different environments and contexts for learning, accredited courses, non-accredited courses that value 'soft targets' such as confidence building.
4   Making a positive contribution
     Volunteering in the community: for example, learners on an access to health course may volunteer at the local hospital. Other avenues include the Duke of

Edinburgh award scheme, community projects, environmental projects, peer mentoring and tutoring. Mentoring can also be carried out online: an example of this is the 'buddy system' that is run by the Helena Kennedy Foundation (an organization that provides financial bursaries, mentoring and support to disadvantaged students from the further and adult education sectors).

5   Achieving economic well-being
Projects with business volunteers, visits to places of work, work-related curriculum activities, Aim Higher projects, Young Enterprise, embedding language, literacy and numeracy (LLN) and ICT into the vocational areas.

An alternative perspective: the rise of therapeutic education

Here is a short extract from an article published a few years ago in *Studies in the Education of Adults*:

> In further and adult education, initiatives such as 'Learning Prescriptions' offer counselling-based college courses and learning support to adults with mental health and emotional problems, referred by their local doctor. In such initiatives, concerns about the low self-esteem of many adults lead to proposals for psychological instruments to diagnose self-esteem and activities to build it. [...] Concern about the emotional well-being of particular groups at all levels of the education system suggests that social and educational inclusion are as much about accommodating people's emotions and providing caring forms of recognition as removing structural or technical barriers to participation and promoting equality. [...] From this perspective, the more that institutions and teachers know about students' psychology, identity and emotional wellbeing, the more inclusive they can be.
>
> (Ecclestone et al., 2005: 186)

In the article, the three authors (Kathryn Ecclestone, Denis Hayes and Frank Furedi) proposed a quite radical critique of aspects of current educational provision throughout both the school and post-school sectors. Ecclestone and Hayes (2008) developed these arguments further in their book *The Dangerous Rise of Therapeutic Education*. They argued that an excessive concentration on the well-being and self-esteem of students and on the need for educational institutions to be at the forefront of a broader social reform agenda have led to a distortion of what education should actually be. Rather than being challenging and stretching (much like many of the experiences faced in 'real life'), schools and colleges were creating artificially cosseted environments: hardly an appropriate way to stimulate learning and fire ambition or enthusiasm. And those who claim that there is too much of an emphasis on 'emotional literacy' (a concept widely written about by journalists and counsellors, but not based on any meaningful educational research) are simply accused of being 'in denial'.

So where do arguments such as this take us? Has a direct focus on the academic or the vocational been replaced by a broader concern for student welfare and well-being?

Has the behaviour of tutors really changed to the extent that they feel unwilling or unable to ask difficult questions of students when in the classroom for fear of being accused of bullying? Is challenging the basis of a student's comment in the classroom really an attack on their self-esteem? Or, to take the challenge directly to the *ECM* agenda, is 'staying safe' leading to students in the LLS being infantilized? Or is it the case that Ecclestone et al. (2005) are in effect arguing for a return to an educational culture where 'what doesn't kill you, makes you stronger', a culture that is best left in the past?

Of course, these are simplifications: the arguments made by Ecclestone et al. are subtle and compelling. And yet it would seem self-evident that the widening participation agenda has been beneficial for many 'non-standard' entrants to programmes of study within the LLS. In our own practice as teacher educators, we have frequently encountered students for whom returning to learning has been beneficial not only in terms of career development, but also in terms of those very issues such as 'self-esteem' and 'confidence', attributes that adult educators have been discussing as being a necessary aspect of learning for a long time before the term 'inclusive practice' became popular. Perhaps, then, what is needed is a more lively debate about 'inclusion', 'emotional literacy' and other related terms. Instead of treating them as dogma, they should be opened up to rigorous scrutiny as part of a critical debate about the role played by educational institutions – in the LLS and elsewhere – in the broader social development of the people who come to them.

Conclusion

The rhetorics of the 'third way', where neoliberalism is at the heart of education, is a challenge when considering widening participation. The language of education including widening participation is based on business terminology where terms such as 'outcomes' are used to measure success. Within educational outcomes there is the idea that all individuals are entrepreneurs managing their own life and responsible for their success or lack of it. The enterprise culture, which requires a continual reconstruction of self to keep up with the changing face of work life, offers a simplistic notion of reinvention. Problems arise as this notion relies on the possibilities a learner has, these possibilities not being equal. The notion of autonomy does not recognize the structural inequalities faced by many learners and the communities in which they live. The discourse of a neoliberal approach to learning societies privileges individual over collective learning. This positions education as a commodity, and pays no regard to issues of economic, political and social equality. The main role given to education is to provide a flexible, adaptable and skilled workforce to make countries competitive in the globalized economy. Inequalities can arise from 'choice' of schooling, the streaming or banding of students, and the nature of the curriculum (discussed in more depth in Chapter 6). These and other factors serve to prepare children from different social classes to enter employment at different levels of organizations: the organization of schooling and work knitted together to perpetuate the inequalities in the class system.

When considering widening participation, critical education and approaches can play a vital role in assisting the progression of marginalized communities and the learners from those communities who are excluded and disadvantaged due to factors such as being poor, ill, unemployed and unqualified, and so on. Emancipatory learning (a theoretical approach that is somewhat out of fashion today) can nonetheless play a role. It allows a shift from the idea that Freire (2000) referred to as the 'banking approach' where learners are viewed as the recipients of knowledge and history, rather than the makers of their history and future. It encourages autonomy and critical thinking, opening up spaces where learners and communities can ask questions, analyse and subsequently work through effective and meaningful strategies to enhance their situation. Rather than being pawns in the system, they have the opportunity to be actors in their future and active members of their communities.

References

Department for Business Innovation and Skills (BIS) (2009) *Skills for Growth: A National Strategy for Economic Growth and Individual Prosperity*. London: BIS.

Department for Children, Schools and Families (DCSF) (2006) *Raising Skills, Improving Life Chances*. London: DCSF.

Department for Education and Skills (DfES) (2004) *Every Child Matters: Change for Children*. Nottingham: DfES.

Ecclestone, K. and Hayes, D. (2008) *The Dangerous Rise of Therapeutic Education*. London: Routledge.

Ecclestone, K., Hayes, D. and Furedi, F. (2005) Knowing me, knowing you: the rise of therapeutic professionalism in the education of adults, *Studies in the Education of Adults*, 37(2): 182–200.

Freire, P. (2000) *Pedagogy of the Oppressed*, 80th anniversary edn. New York: Continuum.

Gee, J., Hull, G. and Lankshear, C. (1996) *The New Work Order: Beyond the Language of the New Capitalism*. St Leonard's: Allen & Unwin.

Higher Education Funding Council for England (HEFCE) (1997a) *The Report of the National Committe of Enquiry into Higher Education*. London: HEFCE.

Higher Education Funding Council for England (HEFCE) (1997b) *The Kennedy Report: Widening Participation in Further Education*. London: HEFCE.

HM Government (2006) *Working Together to Safeguard Children*. London: TSO.

Lifelong Learning UK (LLUK) (2006) *New Overarching Professional Standards for Teachers, Tutors and Trainers in the Lifelong Learning Sector*. London: LLUK.

Lifelong Learning UK (LLUK) (1998) *The Learning Age: A Renaissance for a New Britain*. London: LLUK.

Reay, D., Miriam, E., and Ball, S. (2005) *Degrees of Choice: Social Class, Race and Gender in Higher Education*. Stoke-on-Trent: Trentham Books.

Thomas, L. (2001) *Widening Participation in Post-compulsory Education*. London: Continuum.

Victoria Climbié Report (2003) Available online at www.publications.parliament.uk/palcm200203/cmselect/. . ./570.pdf

3 Policy and practice in the lifelong learning sector

Chapter objectives

This chapter aims to introduce readers to a number of current and recent political debates within the lifelong learning sector (LLS). Through a focus on the politics that lie behind a small number of case studies that are relevant to practitioners, it illustrates how political debates and disagreements shape the working lives of tutors in quite profound ways.

Professional standards

This chapter addresses the following professional practice standards for Qualified Teacher Learning and Skills (QTLS):

> **AK 2.1** **Ways in which learning has the potential to change lives.**
> **AK 2.2** **Ways in which learning promotes the emotional, intellectual, social and economic well-being of individuals and the population as a whole.**
> **AK 6.1** **Relevant statutory requirements and codes of practice.**
> **AK 6.2** **Ways to apply relevant statutory requirements and the underpinning principles.**
>
> (LLUK, 2006)

Introduction

The impact of policy can sometimes be difficult for practitioners to appreciate fully. In some senses, the lived reality of the workshop or classroom seems a world away from those governmental departments that work at local or national level. The actions, motives and even the language of politics are very different from the kinds of issue, activity or decisions that we are normally involved with. And while decisions about funding or qualifications reform are of obvious importance to classroom practitioners, the effects of policy shifts can sometimes take time to filter down to grass roots level.

The relationship between government decisions and public finance seems to be the most obvious way to begin to approach policy, not least because headlines relating to cuts in funding are so easy to find. As this book was being written, the then Labour Government announced significant changes to the ways in which provision for adult learners in the learning and skills sector was to be funded. This in turn followed on from a number of previous announcements relating to significant cuts in funding for the higher education (HE) sector. Perhaps, unsurprisingly, bearing in mind the prevailing economic climate, these stories were reported on in depth in both the mainstream media and in specialist education magazines and papers. Arguments from colleges, universities and student groups relating to the need to invest more heavily in education and training in order to tackle the economic downturn were countered by government statements that reminded us of the significant increases in education spending that had been implemented since 1997. These increases, the government argued, had contributed to record levels of recruitment and achievement that in turn were in line with government targets that related to vocational and technical education, basic and key skills, and participation in HE.

The impact of policy

It is important to remember that it is not actually all about the money even if that is how it feels sometimes. The recent cuts in funding adult learners within the further education (FE) sector (we return to this subject shortly) deserve to be understood in the context of wider political and economic arguments. This is not so say that current or future students – and tutors – will not be affected by these, or other, changes in funding. People who work in the FE sector are very well acquainted with changes in policy that impact more or less immediately on classroom practice (this subject is also returned to later). In order to understand fully the rationale behind particular funding cuts, we also need to consider the policy decisions that lie behind both the reasons for those cuts, and the reasons why those sums of money were there in the first place.

FE colleges increasingly deal with a wide constituency of students: 14–16s, 16–19s and over-19s. As such, they draw down funding from a variety of bodies (which themselves have gone through various incarnations over recent years) that in turn are answerable to two different government departments that have quite specific remits. Responsibilities for education and training were split across two departments in 2007 and this division was maintained after the creation of the Department for Business, Innovation and Skills (BIS), and the Department for Children, Schools and Families (DCSF) which was renamed the Department of Education after the 2010 general election. BIS is responsible for all post-19 education and training, a remit that includes universities and Train to Gain (a strategy to improve the qualifications of the workforce across different areas of trade and industry). With HE in FE representing a significant component of the current government's commitment to widening participation in HE, and with colleges working closely with businesses as part of Train to Gain, BIS is clearly an important stakeholder within the FE sector. Responsibility for students aged 14–19, however, rests with the Department of Education. As such, the Department of Education is also responsible for the oversight of a range of initiatives including the introduction of the 14–19 Diplomas (and the 14–19 Agenda more generally), Functional Skills and *Every Child Matters (ECM)*.

However, the organization that is most pertinent to this current debate regarding funding has begun operating in what are arguably the most difficult financial conditions for a generation. On 1 April 2010, a new body called the Skills Funding Agency (SFA) took over the management of the funding of provision for adult learners within the FE sector. And it would appear, according to recent coverage in the mainstream media, that the new SFA will be assuming its responsibilities at a difficult time.

Case study: cutting funding for adult learners in further education

Colleges, by far the biggest providers of vocational training in Britain, face a £200 million cut to funding for adult students. They have been told 'adult learner responsive' budgets will shrink by 10–25%. Colleges tell us the courses affected include:

- bricklaying, joinery, plastering, plumbing, painting and tiling
- electrical installation
- catering and care – including professional hospitality awards and safe handling of medicines for care workers
- A levels and GCSEs for adults
- qualifications for youth workers
- security, hospitality and licensing
- qualifications in paralegal administration
- IT help desk/junior technician courses
- aeronautical engineering
- Certificate in British Sign Language.

(AOC, 2010)

It could be argued that ever since FE colleges were incorporated (17 years ago), working conditions for lecturers have been characterized by insecurity and casualization: that is, lecturers in FE colleges do not tend to enjoy the same job security that schoolteachers often have. For example, many lecturers work on temporary contracts, or even on an hourly-paid basis. And for tutors in adult education, historically a predominantly part-time and short-term career that is often taken up by people who neither want nor aspire to working full time for a variety of reasons, volatility of employment has long been a concern. Put simply, for tutors in further and adult education, long-term job security is not all that easy to come by. So, in a sense, the announcement of significant cuts to adult learner provision, accompanied by warnings of course closures and job losses, is nothing novel or surprising. This is not to dismiss the problem or to try to diminish its impact. Rather, the point we wish to make is that such an unsettled environment, for tutors as well as learners, is hardly new. Indeed, the resilience of many tutors in the LLS, who continue to want to work with some of the most at risk or vulnerable learners as well as learners who are receiving a second or even third chance, is at times quite remarkable.

Nonetheless, the projected cuts to adult learner provision need to be considered in the light of other recent changes to funding priorities. Over the last few years, the amount of money spent on 16–18 learners within the LLS has increased; at the same time, new forms of provision for adult learners such as Train to Gain have been introduced. As such, the total amount spent on adult learner provision within a FE college has reduced in size, compared to the amount of money spent overall, in recent years. For some colleges, the amount of income that is generated by adult learners is almost zero, for others, over one-third (AOC, 2010). Much of what the FE sector does will not be affected. But those areas of provision that will be affected include literacy, numeracy and English for speakers of other languages (ESOL) (but not courses that impact on the government's Skills For Life targets); trade union education; and some provision for students with disabilities and learning difficulties. In a statement dated 2 February 2010, the General Secretary of the University and College Union (UCU), Sally Hunt, stated that:

> The government has rightly identified education as a key driver of social mobility. However, making swingeing cuts to adult learning now would be an outrageous affront to the millions of people it has promised it would not let down.

It is fair to say that recent governments did indeed position education as a key driver of social mobility, and much education policy has been shaped with this in mind (we return to this later in this chapter). But the fact of having to cope with the fallout of funding changes – or any other rapid changes to government targets or emphasis – is, as we have already suggested, nothing new.

Focus on research: coping with endless change

'Endless change in the learning and skills sector: the impact on teaching staff', a research article written by Sheila Edward, Frank Coffield, Richard Steer and Maggie Gregson (Edward et al., 2007), was published three years ago (that is, well before the kinds of issue that we have discussed so far in this chapter). The article considered the impact of a number of then current policy-led changes including:

1   The restructuring of the Learning and Skills Council (LSC)
2   The Foster review of FE colleges
3   The establishment of the new Quality Improvement Agency (QIA)
4   The Leitch review of skills.

As part of a much larger research project, a part of which was then introduced into Edward et al.'s article, they spoke with teaching and management staff at all stages in their careers: some were new to the sector, and others had worked in FE for over 30 years. One of the conclusions that they arrived at was:

> . . . for most of the tutors we interviewed, the ultimate sources of policy changes were unclear, and mattered little to them, because policy-making was seen as something that happened at a great distance from them, to which they had no input. They lived with the consequences of policy decisions, but could control neither the content nor the pace of these changes.
>
> (Edward et al., 2007: 161)

If we return to the four themes listed above, we find that there has been little respite in the pace of change since this article was published. The LSC is about to be replaced: the Skills Agency which, together with local authorities, will be responsible for 16–19-year-old learners. The QIA was replaced in 2008 by the Learning and Skills Improvement Service (LSIS), which also took over the work previously done by the Centre for Excellence in Leadership (CEL). The Foster review meanwhile can perhaps be seen as starting to have a benign effect. The 14–19 Agenda can in part be seen as a response to what Foster identified as a need for 'a national learning model . . . so that FE's role is constructively co-located alongside HE and schools' (Foster, 2005: viii). And the Leitch review of skills can also be seen as one of the drivers behind the 14–19 Agenda, which in turn has been accompanied by a number of new initiatives and curricular reforms such as the new 14–19 Diplomas, or the move away from Key Skills towards Transferable Skills.

But to what extent is any of this relevant to the working lives of tutors in the sector? It is fairly easy for trainee teachers, when writing assignments for their CertEd/PGCE or DTLLS modules, to mention Leitch (2006) or the 14–19 Agenda. For those tutors who are working towards BA degrees, the study of education policy is quite common. Trying to remember whether or not a particular kind of college- or community-based provision has been brought into existence as a consequence of Leitch HM Treasury (2006), or Foster (2005), or any of the other reports that bear the names of the people who led them (the Warnock Report, 1978; the Kennedy Report HEFCE, 1997b; the Moser Report, DfES, 1999; the Dearing Report, 1997b) is a pretty thankless task. Add to these the various initiatives that have come and sometimes gone over recent years (Skills for Life; Curriculum 2000; the New Deal), and the picture becomes more confusing still. Amid all the publications, policies and initiatives, it can be hard to see the wood for the trees.

A broader analysis: education and politics since 1944

So far we have looked at a number of specific examples of how policy impacts on practice. The themes explored are all relatively current, and continue to have an impact on contemporary teaching practices. At the same time, it is important to be aware of some of those more long-standing political arguments and decisions that over the last

50 years or so have had a profound impact on how education and training provision is organized in the UK. A straightforward way to approach this would be to consider the history of education and training since a little before the end of World War Two. Many excellent books have been written on the subject of the history of education in the twentieth and twenty-first centuries, and we do not intend seriously to add to this body of literature in just one short chapter: rather, we focus on some key pieces of legislation, and then highlight those themes that continue to be meaningful and relevant to practitioners in the LLS today.

1 The 1944 Education Act: the 11-plus

The 1944 Education Act was responsible for the introduction of universal secondary schooling. Until that time, only about 20 per cent of children stayed in formal education after the age of 14, whereas under this new legislation, children would stay in school until age 15, attending one of three kinds of school. The Education Act established three different kinds of school, the idea being that children would be most suited to attending one of the three. After taking an examination when aged 11 (the 11-plus), children could then be directed towards the kind of education that was most appropriate to them. The three kinds of school were:

- grammar schools
- technical schools
- secondary modern schools.

But as time went on, many drawbacks and objections to this system emerged. The 11-plus system of selection favoured middle-class children over working-class children, and did not provide for the kind of social mobility that the architects of the policy had anticipated. Moreover, there is a clear pedagogic concern relating to the validity and reliability of any kind of assessment of children when aged 11 that goes on to restrict their educational opportunities.

The relevance of the 1944 Education Act today

Why is a piece of legislation from nearly 70 years ago still important today to practitioners in the LLS? For those of us who work with adult learners (and this might be in adult or community education, access to HE or accredited HE provision for adults), meeting people who failed the 11-plus and who still feel something akin to shame, or failure, or injustice, or a sense of missed opportunities, is far from uncommon. The 'second chance' that the LLS is able to provide can for some such learners lead to significant change in work, family life and self-esteem.

2 The 1968 Education Act: comprehensive schools

Although the 11-plus system was changed over time, the perceived injustices of the system led the Labour Government of the mid-1960s to embark on a further programme of educational reform. This time the focus was on providing a kind of schooling that would be suitable for everybody. Instead of dividing children into one of three different kinds of school, thereby influencing their longer-term career and life chances, they would go to the same kind of school that would provide a comprehensive education for all.

Changing all schools to comprehensive schools was never, in fact, a uniform process across the country. Rather, it was provided for the first time in 1965 as an option for local authorities to take advantage of what was then reaffirmed in the 1968 Act. The change to a Conservative Government in 1970, followed by the relatively rapid changes of administration in the mid-1970s, meant that the emphasis placed on the comprehensive system also changed. As a result, forms of selection could be maintained in many schools in different parts of the country until the Education Act of 1976 that formally abolished admission by selection in any school funded by the state.

The relevance of the 1968 Education Act today

Despite the proliferation of other kinds of school (we return to this shortly) and the survival of grammar schools in some parts of the country, parts of those broader principals of a universal education, available to all, have proved to be remarkably resilient. Forty years later there is the argument that education can and should be a driver for social reform and social justice, a sentiment that is commonly found among practitioners in the lifelong learning sector (and particularly, in our experience, among tutors of basic and key skills!)

3 The 1988 Education Act: the national curriculum and parental choice

In 1988, the then Conservative Government introduced a wholesale reform of the school curriculum. The introduction of the national curriculum, and to a lesser extent the change from O-levels to GCSEs, are the subjects of many other books and articles and need little discussion here. But as well as introducing curricular reform, the government also introduced a market approach to education as well. Allowing market forces (parental choice, a 'buyers' market') to shape educational provision was representative of the broader ideological approach followed by the government of the time. And the argument was quite simple: if parents had been given the right information about schools, then they could choose which one to send their children to. The good schools would survive and prosper, and the bad ones would either improve or close down. And so the government allowed schools more say in how they spent their funds, and introduced a number of procedures (league tables, Ofsted inspections) that would generate the kind of information that parents would need so that they could make their choice.

The relevance of the 1988 Education Act today

Why is a reform programme that was aimed so squarely at compulsory schooling, not the post-16 sector, relevant for LLS practitioners today? The answer is not to do with technicalities or practicalities, although aspects of the work done by some tutors in the sector are indeed affected (e.g. those tutors who work with learners aged 14–16). Rather, it is to do with the broader political beliefs or ideologies that were introduced by the Conservative Government from 1979 onwards, which were at the heart of the 1988 Education Act, and that were enthusiastically taken up by the Labour Government who came to power in 1997.

4 The 1992 Further and Higher Education Act

Until the early 1990s, FE colleges had been under the control of local authorities. In 1992, the then Conservative Government extended its 'free market' approach to the post-16 sector by allowing colleges to break away from local authority control and be incorporated as, effectively, independent businesses led by a chief executive. Colleges would enjoy the same levels of financial autonomy that schools had been given, and would be subject to the same pressures to maintain recruitment levels. The single biggest impact on teaching staff in colleges was the change to working conditions that had previously been uniform across the sector, but would now be agreed at a local level. New contracts were introduced only after some bitter industrial disputes. Many members of staff in FE now found themselves taking on significantly higher teaching workloads. Pay scales were altered, often to the detriment of staff, and more part-time and temporary staff employed. Teaching staff became used to having to work flexibly. This does not mean that they had to work in the evening, for example (in fact, evening class provision has been gradually eroding over the last 20 years and many colleges are significantly less busy in the evening than they used to be). Rather, it was in the kinds of teaching work required of them that 'flexibility' was increasingly asked for. Teaching new courses to new groups of students, sometimes in subject areas in which they were not familiar, became a common feature of teachers' lives.

It is important to remember that working conditions within FE colleges have not been shaped solely by incorporation, or by the entrenchment of a market model in education that was begun by the Thatcher Government in 1979. Other political and ideological drivers (such as the widening participation agenda, or Skills for Life) have made themselves felt in the FE workplace, and continue to do so. At the same time, working practices across other industrial and business sectors have been shaped by similar ideologies.

The relevance of the 1992 Further and Higher Education Act today

Arguably, the FE sector has continued to be in something of a state of flux since 1992. New initiatives continue to come thick and fast. Working conditions continue to compare unfavourably with sixth-form colleges, secondary or primary schools, although there are high hopes in some circles for the Institute for Learning and the QTLS agenda. Working relationships between teaching staff and college management teams continue to be somewhat disharmonious, although the worst excesses of incorporation appear to have been left behind (that said, occasional cases of mismanagement, accompanied by resignations and occasional prosecutions, do still occur). Perhaps the single most important aspect of the Act that still resonates today is the impact that it had on working conditions. Full-time tutors are routinely expected to teach for at least 25 hours each week, without the ring-fenced planning, preparation and assessment time that schoolteachers enjoy. And there continue to be many other demands on a tutor's time, ranging from the administrative to the pastoral. These demands, juxtaposed to the emotional labour practitioners invest in their working week, such as seeing and supporting learners in unaccounted time slots (e.g. lunch breaks) can leave tutors feeling exhausted and devalued.

The politics of becoming a teacher in the LLS

When writing this book, we anticipated that many (though by no means all) of the readers would be teachers in FE colleges, adult education centres and the like, who were either currently enrolled on or had recently completed a teacher-training course for the post-compulsory sector such as a CertEd, PGCE, or a PTLLS, CTLLS or DTLLS award, endorsed by LLUK. Teaching qualifications such as these are now compulsory for new entrants to the profession, although for many years this was not the case. In addition, the successful completion of an in-service award (i.e. studying for a CertEd on a part-time basis while in paid employment within the sector) is often a contractual obligation. So, why is initial teacher training for the post-compulsory sector relevant to this current discussion of policy? The answer is simple: an appreciation of why initial teacher training is now obligatory, and linked to a series of professional standards, sheds further light on a number of the policy discussions that we have already explored.

FENTO, LLUK and the journey towards professional standards

The Further Education National Training Organisation (FENTO) began operating in 1998, in the same year that the then Labour Government had called for a more comprehensive approach to the training of teachers for the LLS. Before this time, teacher training within the sector had been somewhat disparate. This is not to say that the curriculum for teacher training was chaotic or insufficient: far from it. Many universities offered CertEd/PGCE courses, and other awarding bodies offered their own qualifications (such as the City and Guilds 7307 Further and Adult Education Teachers Certificate). And there was an established body of literature relating to teaching and learning in the sector (although it must be acknowledged that this has grown considerably over recent years). The following year, FENTO (1999) published the *Standards For Teaching and Supporting Learning in Further Education In England and Wales*. The standards set out the skills and knowledge that were deemed essential to the role of the teacher or trainer in FE. What the FENTO standards provided for the first time was a *national* framework that could be recognized as providing a sector-wide body of standards. And from 2001, all teacher-training qualifications would have to cover these standards in order to be shown to be sufficient and appropriate. At the same time, it is important to note that a similar process, relating to the training of primary and secondary school teachers, had already begun with the creation of the Council for the Accreditation of Teacher Education in 1984 (superseded first by the Teacher Training Agency, and now the Training and Development Agency for Schools).

After a few years, it was decided that the FENTO standards would be replaced with a new set of professional standards that would more adequately reflect the diversity of the LLS as a whole, rather than focusing on FE colleges. In addition, the old FENTO standards were perceived as being suitable as standards for already qualified and ex-perienced tutors, but perhaps of less value when used as outcomes for initial teacher training programmes. From 1 January 2005 a new organization, LLUK, began operating as the body responsible for – among other things – the professional development of all employees in the field of lifelong learning. A subsidiary organization called Standards Verification UK took over the role of approving and endorsing teacher training qual-ifications in the post-compulsory sector that was once carried out by FENTO, which ceased to exist. In the previous year, the DfES (2004) published a document called *Equipping our Teachers for the Future: Reforming Initial Teacher Training for the Learning and Skills Sector*. This document set out a timetable for changes to teacher training in the post-16 sector that culminated in a new range of qualifications, backed up by a new set of occupational standards (the *New Professional Standards for Teachers, Tutors and Trainers in the Lifelong Learning Sector*), which replaced the old FENTO standards in 2007.

Equipping our Teachers also proposed the establishment of a professional body for teachers and trainers in the LLS. Consequently, the Institute for Learning (IfL) was estab-lished in 2007, and serves to represent the collective interests of this varied group of pro-fessionals. It also serves to provide professional recognition for practitioners, through the monitoring and awarding of QTLS/ATLS status for teachers. Continuing profes-sional development (CPD), a mandatory requirement for full- and part-time teachers, provides the mechanism through which QTLS/ATLS status is conferred and falls under the purview of the IfL.

Professional standards: some critical perspectives

This all might seem at first glance to be an entirely sensible process of standardizing teacher-training programmes as part of a broader quality assurance process. But there are in fact some significant political debates and disagreements at work here. In the early 1980s, teacher-training curricula were criticized by the government, teachers and trainee teachers, and some academics for being out of touch with classroom practice. The establishment of those organizations that would endorse such qualifications in the future (i.e. first FENTO and now LLUK) would therefore help the curriculum become more responsive to the needs of the profession, rather than being 'too academic' and divorced from classroom reality. And Ofsted, which had its remit expanded to cover the LLS in 2000, would be able to inspect the quality of such provision and find out which programmes, if any, were not fit for purpose and therefore not deserving of public funding.

But there are two important criticisms to be raised here. The first is that the real reason why teacher training was taken out of the hands of universities and placed under the control of central government (via Ofsted, LLUK and other organizations) was not to do with ensuring quality or standardization, but related to an ideologically-driven desire to attack the professionalism and independence of universities and teachers more generally. The main reason why these structures and systems were brought into being was not because of any anticipated improvement in the quality or provision of teacher training as such; rather, they were brought into being as part of that same broad ideological push from the then Conservative Government that led to the incorporation of colleges and the growth of a market model in lifelong learning.

The second criticism relates to the creation of professional standards themselves. Is it possible to capture the richness and complexities that make up the work of a teacher in the LLS in a series of bullet points? The earlier FENTO standards were acknowledged by the government as being inadequate. But are the new LLUK standards any better at setting appropriate benchmarks for what a teacher knows and does? Being able to list or codify what professionals know and how they go about doing their work is in fact a complex task from both a practical and a theoretical point of view. What it means to 'know something' or to be 'knowledgeable' is a matter of considerable scholarly debate (Tummons, 2009). Part of this debate includes striving for critical awareness of one's reality whereby practitioners strive for authenticity in their practice.

Focus on research: from teaching standards to teaching practice

'Translating national standards into practice for the initial training of Further Education (FE) teachers in England', a research article written by Tony Nasta (2007), was written at the time when the transition from FENTO to LLUK was under way. In the article, Nasta raised this same crucial theoretical point relating to professional standards. Drawing on the theories of writers such as Michael Eraut and Michael Polanyi, he questioned the extent to which any set of professional standards (and not just a set written for teachers) might be able adequately to capture or represent the knowledge, experience and abilities that professionals possess. He also questioned the extent to which the professional practices and understanding of such a varied sector could adequately be captured in a single body of standards. Here, he drew attention not only to obvious differences between adult education provision and mainstream FE, for example, but also to the differences that might be found even within similar institutions. FE colleges, for example, are hardly homogeneous: they often have particular specialisms or areas of excellence, sometimes dating back many years. Moreover, depending on where they are located, they may serve very different student populations. In effect, there is no such thing as a 'typical' FE college: so how can there be a single set of professional standards? (Nasta, 2007.)

Task: reflecting on professional standards

The original FENTO standards were replaced in 2007 partly because they were seen as being insufficiently representative of the diversity of the LLS as a whole. In addition, they placed insufficient emphasis on subject specialist pedagogies, and on 14–16 education and training (Ofsted, 2004). So to what extent do you think that the new LLUK standards are more relevant for trainee teachers in the sector? Have they helped to generate a broader discussion about professionalism and professional values among the teaching workforce? Have they simply become another checklist item for teacher-training students to consider when compiling their portfolios? Have they been lost sight of among all the other things that teachers and trainers need to know and do on a daily basis?

Conclusion

Politics is a big subject, and the politics of the LLS are diverse and complex. Any number of themes or issues could have been explored in a chapter of considerably greater length than this one. Possible areas for further research might be the impact of policy on adult basic skills provision or on offender learning. What we have tried to show in this chapter is that there is more to an understanding of policy in the LLS than simply remembering which initiative or report happened when. The philosophies and ideologies that underpin the work of different governments do not just exist at an abstract theoretical level. They are real, and they make a difference to the jobs that we do. As practitioners in the LLS, we can often feel disempowered by institutional and external pressures that can erode our autonomy, undermine our integrity and challenge authentic approaches to our practice. Actions and ideologies from a long time ago continue to make themselves felt, and new initiatives and political beliefs emerge with such frequency that as practitioners we almost feel swamped by them. Perhaps that's the idea?

References

Association of Colleges (AOC) (2010) *AOC Funding Survey Number 1: Adult Learning Funding.* Available online www.aoc.co.uk/download.cfm?docid=8A4C4B4A-9D19-49EC-9E58662080097DBE

Department for Education and Skills (DfES) (1999) *A Fresh Start: Improving Literacy and Numeracy.* Available online at www.dfes.gov.uk/afreshstart

Department for Education and Skills (DfES) (2004) *Equipping our Teachers for the Future: Reforming Initial Teacher Training for the Learning and Skills Sector.* London: DfES.

Edward, S., Coffield, F., Steer, R. and Gregson, M. (2007) Endless change in the learning and skills sector: the impact on teaching staff, *Journal of Vocational Education and Training*, 59(2): 155–73.

Foster, A. (2005) *Realising the Potential: a Review of the Future Role of Further Education Colleges*. Annesley: Department for Education and Skills (DfES).

Further Education National Training Organisation (FENTO) (1999) *Standards for Teaching and Supporting Learning in Further Education in England and Wales*. London: FENTO.

Her Majesty's Stationery Office (1978) *The Warnock Report*. London: HMSO.

Higher Education Funding Council for England (HEFCE) (1997a) *The Report of the National Committee of Enquiry into Higher Education*. London: HEFCE.

Higher Education Funding Council for England (HEFCE) (1997b) *The Kennedy Report: Widening Participation in Further Education*. London: HEFCE.

HM Treasury (2006) *The Leitch Review of Skills*. London: HM Treasury.

Lifelong Learning UK (LLUK) (2006) *New Overarching Professional Standards for Teachers, Tutors and Trainers in the Lifelong Learning Sector*. London: LLUK.

Nasta, T. (2007) Translating national standards into practice for the initial training of further education (FE) teachers in England, *Research in Post-Compulsory Education*, 12(1): 1–17.

Ofsted (2004) *The Initial Training of Further Education Teachers: A Survey*. London: Ofsted.

Tummons, J. (2009) *Curriculum Studies in the Lifelong Learning Sector*. Exeter: Learning Matters.

4 Embedding literacy, numeracy and information and communication technology

Chapter objectives

This chapter looks at a proposed theoretical approach that includes social practice accounts of literacy/language, numeracy (LLN) and information and communication technology (ICT). It explores working with the new core curriculum together with identifying strategies for embedding LLN and ICT. To support this it considers critical approaches to teaching and learning Skills for Life.

Professional standards

This chapter addresses the following professional practice standards for Qualified Teacher Learning and Skills (QTLS):

AK 1.1 **What motivates learners to learn and the importance of learners' experiences and aspirations.**

BK 2.5 **Ways of using learners' own experience as a foundation for learning.**

CK 3.3 **The different ways in which language, literacy and numeracy skills are integral to learners' achievement in own specialist area.**

CK 3.4 **The language, literacy and numeracy skills required to support own specialist teaching.**

CK 3.5 **Ways to support learners in the use of new and emerging technologies in own specialist area.**

(LLUK, 2006)

Introduction

Adult literacy and numeracy provision is an established component of vocational education and training in the UK. As such the politics of curriculum, including LLN is a key issue for policy makers, theorists, managers and practitioners. The model of curriculum can determine whether education is an emancipating or suppressing process. As such, the lifelong curriculum, which includes *Skills for Life* (SfL),[1] may be situated not as neutral or apolitical but at the centre of educational power. For example, in an age of globalization and neoliberalism, it may be viewed as a product of market-driven changes, where approaches to Skills for Life involve a functional literacy approach. This is defined by its social purposes in which there is an alignment between individual skills, the performance of society, the global economy and economic productivity. Easily testable outcomes, such as the Skills for Life end tests, are often what the lifelong learning sector (LLS) follows to measure performance, pull down funding and beat national benchmarks. Deficits are measured against a fixed and discrete set of transferable skills. The curriculum is not static; it changes to meet the demands of a market-driven culture and as a result of the requirements of competition. What it fails to recognize and address is the historical and contemporary disparities that exist in the structural inequalities between the learners and their lives, for example, class, gender and ethnicity.

Approaches to literacy

As identified in the *Teaching and Learning Research Briefing*, 'Harnessing everyday literacies for student learning at college' (Ivanic et al. 2008: 1) 'Literacy is a significant factor affecting retention, progression and achievement in colleges'. The study identified how the span of literacy practices in college was less than that which the students engaged in their everyday life. The literacy practices were driven and captured by 'wash back effect' from assessment regimes. The implications were that the everyday literacy practices of the learners were often invisible and not valued as skills that they could bring into the classroom to support learning in a more holistic way. The study recommended that:

> Lecturers can use an understanding of literacy as a set of social practices to fine-tune their pedagogy. They can make small changes in practice which aim to make reading and writing on courses more resonant with students' vernacular literacy practices, make the student more aware of reading and writing in their everyday lives which could act as a resource for their learning, make the communicative aspects more explicit and visible, and make the reading and writing on courses more relevant to learning.

---

[1] *A Fresh Start : Improving Literacy and Numeracy,* produced by a working group chaired by Sir Claus Moser (DfES, 1999), recommended that a national strategy for adult basic skills was developed to begin to address literacy and numeracy skills needs. It had ambitious targets for reducing the number of adults with low skills levels. The Moser Report drew on some of the evidence in the survey to estimate that approximately 20 per cent of the UK population (as many as seven million people) apparently had difficulty with functional literacy and/or numeracy. This was defined as 'the ability to read, write and speak in English and use mathematics at a level necessary to function at work and in society in general'. The resulting strategy, *Skills for Life* (DfES, 2001), identified a number of priority groups that included people who live in disadvantaged communities. The Leitch review (HM Treasury, 2006) has indicated the subsequent steps for the Skills for Life strategy that recommends the UK commit to becoming a world leader in skills.

A way to address the above is to move towards a model based on a socially situated approach. Social approaches to literacy are sometimes grouped together under the remit of the New Literacy Studies (NLS) (Street, 1984; Barton, 1994; Gee, 1996; Barton and Hamilton, 1998). Within this complex view of the nature of literacy, we can highlight that literacy has many purposes for the learner. It challenges the dominance of the autonomous model, and recognizes how literacy practices vary from one cultural and historical context to another. These literacy practices provide a focus and methodology whereby there is a close proximity between literacy practices, identities and discourse and how literacy practices both in the private domain of home and in the public domain of formal education are shaped by power and ideology so that literacy is configured differently in a different context. This focus can support tutors to shift from a narrow competency-based approach, which separates the literacies from their context, and instead to harness the everyday practices learners bring into the classroom. As such, literacy is not just a technical or neutral skill; it provides a social view that is expanded by treating literacy as not only a social practice but also as a multimodal form of communication. It recognizes music, images, symbols and other forms of expression as being literacy practices. The use of multimodal literacies offers the expansion of the ways learners acquire information and understand concepts. Words, images, sound, colour, animation, video and styles of print can be combined. This approach moves from a deficit model of literacies, and instead recognizes that 'language, literacy and numeracy involves paying attention first and foremost to the contexts, purposes and practices in which language (spoken and written) and mathematical operations play a part' (Barton et al., 2007: 17).

Task: identifying literacy domains

Identify the different literacies you use in different settings. Two examples are given in Tables 4.1 and 4.2 as follows:

Table 4.1   Literacies and domains working grid

Domains	Public	Private
Literacy/language	Work – write reports	
Numeracy		Home – work out bills
ICT		

Now consider how you can bring the literacies learners use outside the classroom into the classroom.

You may have considered the items below in Table 4.2. This is not an exhaustive list, and after finding out the interests of your groups see if you can add more. You might want them to do a project on their interests.

Table 4.2 Examples of literacy practices

Home	Shopping – working out prices/writing shopping lists
	Working out bills
	Cooking – reading recipes/measuring ingredients
	Looking after family – organizational skills
Hobbies	Working out football scores/coupons
	Following knitting patterns
	DIY – working out measurements for fitting shelves/decorating
	Crosswords
	Photography
	Art and crafts – e.g. making cards
	Genealogy – researching family tree
Work	Writing memos
	Working in a team
	Voluntary work – e.g. running playgroups, cubs, brownies, etc.

It is generally thought that recognizing the literacies that learners bring into the classroom is an effective strategy to teaching and learning. Purposeful and meaningful learning builds and expands on learners' prior knowledge and experience to shape and construct new knowledge, rather than seeing the learner as an empty vessel ready to be filled by the tutor. Learning is seen as a social activity embedded in particular cultures and contexts where assessment is based on them demonstrating their competency in achieving the specific learning outcomes. Demonstration of the achievement of these learning outcomes is situated in the learners' real life and everyday practices. The teaching and learning resources can be developed by the learner to capture and give meaning to their experience, motivation and aspirations, or co-produced with the teacher, rather than arising from a prescriptive preset curriculum.

Look at the narrative and task in the following case study. It has been developed to support the 'easy read book' written by a former adult literacy learner, Marie McNamara. The aim is for learners to read Marie's motivational story and begin to plan their progression routes.

Case study: supporting literacy learning

Going back to education
was changing all our lives
History was not going to repeat itself
I was making sure of that.
I took another course
called Access to Health and Nursing.
I realised I wanted to be a nurse,
but needed more qualifications

(McNamara, 2007: 9–10)

Example of Resource

Name	_____	Tutor	_____
Date	_____		

2. Your future steps

Think about where you would like to be or what you would like to be doing in 3 years' time. Think about the steps you need to take.

One year

Two years

Three years

Who do you need to contact to help you to take your steps and reach your goals? What do you need to do? Here are some suggestions.

Tutor	Counsellor	Employer
Support worker	Careers guidance	Friends
	Read newspaper	Visit library

Figure 4.1 Planning your future steps

Task

Now, work with one of your learners to produce a resource. You may want to use a piece of their writing; for example, a poem can be turned it into a comprehension. You may also want to ask the learner if you can share their piece of writing and the resource to use with the whole class. This can boost confidence for the learner and be inspirational and motivating for the group.

Impact of literacy education

Literacy education has been shown to enhance confidence, contribute to personal development, promote health, and social and political participation. Literacy courses for young and older adults can offer them a second chance of re-engaging with education; it can contribute to personal development and provides economic and social benefits.

The following case study focuses on Dean who returned to learning following redundancy. He gives an account of how numeracy began to make sense in his daily life.

Case study: learning numeracy

Coming back into education was a big step for me. I had not done that well at school and to be honest I was worried people in college would think I wasn't clever enough to be on a course. I had been made redundant from the warehouse where I'd worked and getting another job had been tough. At first I only went back to get my maths up to scratch. What surprised me was how maths made sense the second time around. I understood the calculations because the tutor related them to my life. So when we covered the topic of 'area' we looked at how this could be applied to the calculations for buying wall-paper and decorating my front room. It began to make sense. Not only did I improve my numeracy skills, but I decorated my front room and now I'm a self employed painter and decorator!

Towards a new skills curriculum

The report *A Fresh Start: Improving Literacy and Numeracy* produced by Sir Claus Moser (DfES, 1999), helped shape the Labour Government's strategy to improve the literacy, numeracy and language skills of adults. While the Leitch report, produced by Lord Leitch in December 2006 (HM Treasury, 2006) called *Prosperity for all in the Global Economy: World Class Skills*, set ambitious goals that impact on Skills for Life. Some of the objectives include:

- 95 per cent of adults to achieve the basic skills of functional literacy and numeracy, an increase from levels of 85 per cent literacy and 79 per cent numeracy in 2005;
- exceeding 90 per cent of adults qualified to at least Level 2, an increase from 69 per cent in 2005. A commitment to go further and achieve 95 per cent as soon as possible;
- shifting the balance of intermediate skills from Level 2 to Level 3. Improving the esteem, quantity and quality of intermediate skills. This means 1.9 million additional Level 3 attainments over the period and boosting the number of Apprentices to 500,000 a year;
- exceeding 40 per cent of adults qualified to Level 4 and above, up from 29 per cent in 2005, with a commitment to continue progression.

(HM Treasury, 2006)

Furthermore, as part of the government's strategy for improving adult basic skills a set of national standards have been developed by the Qualifications and Curriculum Authority (QCA). These summarize the skills and capabilities relating to literacy and numeracy that they deem adults are considered to need in order to function and progress at work, and in wider society more generally. To support this, the new Skills for Life core curriculum was developed by the Learning and Skills Improvement Service (LSIS) and is available via the Excellence Gateway – LSIS's online portal for the further education (FE) sector. Improvements have been made to the existing adult literacy, ESOL (English for speakers of other languages) and numeracy. An interactive facility for tutors of the adult pre-entry curriculum is also available.

The revised curriculum may be used as an interactive tool and aims to:

- promote flexible and creative use of the curriculum content in a variety of learning contexts, including embedded learning
- enhance content and resources with additional guidance, exemplification and vocational material
- provide tools and features that will enable practitioners, including the wider embedded-learning audience, to create effective personal learning experiences
- provide an online community where ideas and innovation can be shared and developed.

(*Source:* www.excellencegateway.org.uk/page.aspx?o=sflcurriculum)

Task: exploring the core curriculum

Go to the online portal and look at the literacy, ESOL and numeracy core curriculum (www.excellencegateway.org.uk/sflcurriculum) and identify the areas covered.
  You may have identified the following (see Table 4.3):

Table 4.3   Summary of basic skills curricula

Curriculum name	What it covers
Adult literacy curriculum	Speaking, listening, reading and writing skills for adults
Adult numeracy curriculum	Numeracy skills for adults
Adult ESOL curriculum	A literacy curriculum for adults learning English as an additional language
Adult pre-entry curriculum	This document provides a curriculum for learners who are not yet at Entry level 1
Access for all curriculum	This document provides advice on how to make the curriculum accessible to learners with other needs, from hearing problems to dyslexia

ICT

Together with LLN, Information and Communication Technology (ICT) now also comes under the national standards and core curriculum. A key driver for this was the 2003 *White Paper, 21st Century Skills: realising our potential* (DfES, 2003), which spoke of the commitment to help adults to develop ICT as a third 'skill for life' alongside literacy and numeracy. To support this, national standards for ICT were published alongside the existing standards for adult literacy and numeracy. The standards for adult literacy and numeracy and ICT follow a common format and relate directly to the key skills of communication, application of number and ICT. Juxtaposed to this they have been developed and implemented to match the national curriculum requirements for English, mathematics, ICT and the national occupational standards for ICT. ICT skills are an important feature of life and work in a contemporary society and are continually evolving. As such the world of work and other activities are increasingly being transformed by access to varied and developing technology. ICT supports learners to acquire and develop the skills to participate. The ICT tools can be used to find, explore, analyse, exchange and present information in a creative way. It enables rapid access to ideas and experiences from a wide range of people, communities and cultures:

> It is now widely accepted that the use of e-learning as part of a blended approach to teaching Skills for Life is highly effective for motivating and engaging learners. Learners like using technology, if they feel it is relevant to their lives, and if they are already using it for life and leisure purposes, then it is vitally important that their teachers know how to integrate it into the teaching and learning process. But this is not always the case. Although many good examples of the use of e-learning in Skills for Life are emerging, many teachers are still not confident about using technology themselves and even less confident about using it in the classroom.
>
> (Hunt, 2005)

Embedding ICT with other SfL subjects is a means to facilitate learners to achieve both standards: that is, ICT with literacy and ICT with numeracy. Used well, ICT is a powerful motivator for many 'hard to reach learners' and linking the subjects can encourage many learners to participate. Mellar et al. (2007: 12) suggest that:

- ICT is a powerful tool to raise levels of literacy and numeracy
- computers and multimedia software provide attractive ways of learning
- the web enables access to the best materials and the most exciting learning opportunities
- ICT offers a new start for adults returning to learning
- the Internet and digital TV technology can reach into the home
- learners who use ICT for basic skills double the value of their study time, acquiring two sets of skills at the same time.

Contextualized learning

Within this model learners are taught core/key/functional skills away from the vocational area. These classes are usually delivered by specialist Skills for Life tutors outside the vocational timetable. The can be delivered in a number of ways that include: workshops, tutorials, taught sessions, group classes and 1:1 support. The tutor aims to make the content of the delivery relevant to the learners' vocational areas. Traditionally, the teaching and learning of skills is maintained as a set of skills that are not socially situated. As such the culture, values and practices of the vocational area do not permeate the teaching and learning of the skills.

As tutors delivering your specialized area, you will need to think about how you can contextualize LLN and ICT into your curriculum and facilitate the development of these practices in your learners. For example:

- visiting websites for suggestions for the types of activity that could be used in vocational subject areas to help learners develop these practices. See www.excellencegateway.org.uk/pdf/Contexts%20for%20non%20specialists.pdf
- consult with their LLN and ICT specialist colleagues
- continuing professional development (CPD)
- partaking in action research
- joining a community of practice.

What is embedded learning?

In the context of the SfL strategy, it may be defined as:

> Embedded teaching and learning combines the development of literacy, language and numeracy with vocational and other skills. The skills acquired provide learners with the confidence, competence and motivation necessary for them to progress, gain qualifications and to succeed in life and at work.
> (www.excellencegateway.org.uk/pdf/Embedding%20def%20&%20sites%20clean%20final%20version%20HS%2023%20Dec.pdf)

Indeed, the teaching of any subject may lead in some manner to using LLN and ICT. For example, the three functional skills of English, mathematics and ICT are part of the new Diplomas, relevant GCSEs and apprenticeships. They will replace the key skills of communication, application of number and ICT. The functional skills standards cover from Entry level 1 to Level 2, and will be extended to Level 3. In the embedded model vocational tutors do not teach discrete core/key/functional skills; they are embedded into that area. It is increasingly important to cover these areas to facilitate learners to develop skills and confidence in LLN and ICT. What is more, in order to progress through courses, an increasing prerequisite is that learners have gained their functional skills at Level 2. See Table 4.4 for an example of progression routes linked to LLN.

Table 4.4 Basic skills requirement for different progression routes

Course	LLN Requirements
Starting point	
Pre-foundation Health and Social Care	No entry qualifications
Foundation Health and Social Care	Level 1 End Tests Literacy/numeracy
Intermediate Health and Social Care	Level 2 End Tests Literacy/numeracy
Advanced Health and Social Care	Level 3 Literacy/numeracy

For learners who have lost their confidence with literacy and numeracy, embedding is a way to place the skills into a context that has meaning to them, their lives and hopes for the future. It can hook them in, particularly when learners often 'can seem incredibly motivated not to be motivated' (Long, 2005: 1). To support this model, it is crucial that tutors understand their learners, their culture and what it is that motivates them. Encouraging the learners to recognize their skill development in the context of their specialism can also be an empowering process whereby they learn to value the literacies they bring to the classroom and use in many aspects of their life.

Task: embedding the core curricula

Consider how you can embed LLN and ICT into your curriculum area. Think about the impact and consequences of embedding LLN and ICT.
     Ways to embed LLN and ICT can include:

- work with LLN specialists, subject learning coaches or other colleagues
- identify spaces in your scheme of work where you can embed LLN and ICT
- visit online sites that have LLN and ICT materials; for example, BBC Skills Wise www.bbc.co.uk/skillswise/read.write.plus   and   www.rwp.excellencegateway. org.uk/readwriteplus/
- work with your learners to develop resources meaningful to them.

And benefits include:

- improved learner retention
- better success rates: Casey et al. (2006) has shown that vocational courses that had LLN embedded had a 26 per cent higher success rate than courses with no embedding
- staff teams who are more confident in developing learners' skills

- learners gain new skills and confidence
- they are better prepared to access and progression into vocational routes
- raising LLN levels can play a key role in improving employment opportunities National Research and Development Centre (NRDC) research shows that a lack of LLN skills can have clear adverse economic consequences (Bynner and Parsons, 2006)
- offers learners the opportunity to express their views/beliefs, describe their challenges and document their success stories (Dolan, 2008).

In the following case study trainee teacher, Lorraine Compton, contextualizes numeracy into a history session:

Case study: embedding numeracy

The session I have planned is centred on the 2004 presidential election in America: Kerry vs. Bush where I have focused and embedded numeracy into the material taught. The emphasis is going to be on realising that Kerry lost the election by a considerable margin, and on preparing the students for a session discussing why this was the case.

Numeracy can be embedded into a session like this in many creative ways. However, often, like the majority of history sessions, due to its disciplined nature as an academic subject, the embedding of numeracy would require a relatively behaviourist approach to learning. The reason for this is that numeracy would have to be acknowledged in the session through the setting of tasks and establishment of structured aims and objectives. Level 2 numeracy is not 'naturally' embedded into history, which is to say it does not occur through the general disciplines history promotes, such as critical analysis. Therefore to adopt a more humanist approach and expect that the learners will be able to develop their Level 2 numeracy through a wide and accomplished understanding of history is unrealistic. What would more likely occur is a disengaging with the subject matter, as it could feel that numeracy had no place there at all.

Disengagement is something that could also occur even with a more behaviourist model if it appears that the numeracy is irrelevant. Rather, I am going to try to adapt a more holistic approach to the embedding of numeracy. This will be done through an appreciation of the cognitive model of learning also, as the numeracy will stand to help resolve historical problems and evidence historical debates, so that the learners can store it, and retrieve it in another situation. The storing and retrieval of information is crucial in the cognitive learning model, and therefore providing I am able to embed numeracy in a natural way into my session, the aim is that students should find this storing and retrieval easy to accomplish.

Table 4.5 The Polling Report (2004)

	ALL %	BUSH voters %	KERRY voters %	Decimal:
Moral values	27	44	7	
Iraq	22	11	34	
Economy/jobs	21	7	36	
Terrorism	14	24	3	
Health care	4	1	8	
Education	4	2	6	
Taxes	3	4	2	
Other (vol.)	4	5	3	
Unsure	1	2	1	

Source: The Polling Report (2004) www.edition.cnn.com/ELECTION/2004/pages/results/electoral. college/ (accessed 12 November 2009).

Examples of using numeracy in a session concerning the 2004 American presidential election can be seen in Table 4.5 (where each activity is numbered).

1)

'Which ONE issue mattered most to you in deciding how you voted for president?'
Using the table of percentages (Table 4.5), discuss in your groups the main issue that mattered to the American people (noting that voters were split between different camps) when voting for who was to become the next president. To help this process, using these percentages work out the decimal of the percentage relating to Kerry to illustrate how considerable, or not, the issue was for his voters. Using both percentages and decimals will help you to more fully visualise the importance of the different aspects.
A little reminder of how to convert from a percentage to a decimal is to remember that 'percent' means 'out of a hundred'

e.g. 34% = 34/100

to convert to decimal then is to do the sum

34/100 which equals 0.34

This task will get students using a table to extract information, as well as working with percentages, fractions and decimals. These are all important features of level 2 numeracy. The task is relevant as it will demonstrate to the students in another mathematical form that Kerry's voters were considerably different to Bush's, which in turn may help to relate to the session that would occur after this as to why this was the case, and therefore why Kerry lost the election race.

2)

Source: www.edition.cnn.com/ELECTION/2004/pages/results/electoral.college/ (accessed 12 November 2009)

Use the information above to create a pie chart comparing and contrasting the numbers that voted Kerry or Bush. This provides you with a clear visual representation of the number of votes involved, which will help you to contrast Bush's winning vote numbers with Kerry's. Is anything interesting revealed here?

This task will require students to extract information from a map, as well as understanding the key to this map. While students are doing this they will be using numeracy to help their understanding of the situation as well as creating a pie chart/ understanding the concept of graphs.

3)

True or false?
Bush won by a margin of 30 rounded to the nearest ten.
Kerry's largest win was 34 in Texas.
Kerry's voters were concerned more about Iraq than the economy.
The difference between Bush's voters caring about education and Kerry's is 0.04.
Bush and Kerry's voters generally agree on the importance of matters.

4)

Using all of the information you have assessed throughout the session, and the tasks you have completed – how successful do you think the Kerry campaign was?

The next session would go on to consider the reasons why the Kerry campaign was not a success, using the knowledge the students have gained from this session – that the campaign was not successful, and that Kerry's voters were very different to Bush's and Bush won by a relative margin.

The numeracy used in this session could be adapted to many other historical situations, not least every presidential election race. However, generally not all these examples would occur in one session. Nevertheless, other ways these could be used include creating pie charts concerning the length each of Henry VIII's wives lived for, turning the percentage of members of British Empire (not including Great Britain) that fought and were killed during World War Two into a fraction and then a decimal, for example. For the students, viewing figures in different numerical ways can help embed the knowledge in their minds, so that they are able to extract it later and use it help solve other problems (for example, in the end of year exam).

The learners

Many learners arrive at classes with domestic and social commitments, and may have overcome significant barriers to gain the confidence and courage to return to learning. Having the space to explore their life and learning narratives and make sense of events that have held them back can help remove the negativity and lead to academic progress and personal fulfilment. The emphasis on developing self-esteem and acknowledging and coming to terms with an array of emotions may also provide a secure and positive environment that can facilitate tutors to engage with learners in egalitarian and critical ways rather than simply controlling them.

Resources: different approaches

High quality and meaningful materials contribute significantly to the quality of the learning experience. Approaches to the design, implementation and evaluation of resources will however vary, depending on the needs of the learners. Functional and cognitive approaches tend to favour standard prescriptive approaches; function-oriented programmes tailor their materials to the different tasks and different situations for which learners require LLN. Social practice models as discussed above and transformative approaches move towards a content that is pulled from local environments and cultural contexts.

A key factor in the development of resources is that they also offer the opportunity for autonomy, whereby the learners are encouraged to think about the actions they need to take to equip them to develop their knowledge and take their skills forward.

To support the development of these skills resources can be shaped by the vocational area the learner wants to progress into. The following (Fig. 4.2) resource is based on the story of James, a car mechanic. It aims to encourage learners to consider

Name		Tutor	
Date		Class	

My Learning Journey So Far

Draw a map of your learning journey and share it with the group. Think about where you are now and the steps you took to get to this point.

Name		Tutor	
Date		Class	

My Future Learning Journey

Draw a map of your future learning journey. You could include an image of something motivational at the centre of the map, for example a picture of your family or friends, an image of someone in the uniform of the career you want to progress onto, a smiling face or an empowering image.

Why don't you keep a journal of your journey? It might help you to identify real barriers and help you put forward actions to address them. You could bring your journal to the lesson to share with others in the group and discuss your progress.

Figure 4.2 My learning journey so far/My future learning journey

numeracy in the context of their specialised area: car mechanics. The second resource aims to facilitate learners' own life situation, their hopes for the future and help them to identify a series of actions they can take towards driving their career goal forward. To fully support and engage the learners' progression, functional skills are embedded into the resources. The resources move from a deficit model of literacy and numeracy where the learner is positioned as 'lacking' and, instead, embraces a model that encourages the learners to recognize and celebrate their knowledge and achievements in the context of their own lives, community and vocational area. Together with developing their personal skills, the resources also seek to promote strategies that support learners to research and apply for jobs and/or progress into further training. Some of the tasks also encourage learners to look at their strengths and areas for development in order to develop a personal action plan. A key factor of the resources is that they offer the opportunity for autonomy, whereby the learners are encouraged to think about the actions they need to take to equip them to develop their knowledge and take their skills forward. Figure 4.3 looks at developing numeracy in the context of record keeping.

Working with learners

Since literacies are highly valued in modern society, and almost everything that people do requires at least a functional level, struggling with LLN and ICT can limit what young people and adults can accomplish. SfL programmes and vocational courses with LLN and ICT addressed can support them in recognizing and developing their skills. However, one obstacle can stand in the way of their success – their embarrassment over their struggle to read, work out numbers, use a computer and their wariness to admit the extent of their problem. The process of facilitating learners to develop their own resources can be highly motivational and ensures that they relate to their needs/interests/aspirations and goals. Resources developed by learners can be used in LLN and ICT programmes in different ways such as:

- published collections of student writing a collection of writing or 'scribed' stories for a book
- contributions to the LLN scheme of work
- reading narratives for a whole group (e.g. poetry – the tutor can use the stories to teach phonics, pointing out and asking the learner to point out patterns and similarities and differences in the words and sounds)
- published small books
- placing the LLN and ICT in the context of their working life (e.g. form filling).

What is more, developing meaningful materials with learners is an excellent method of making more resources accessible at local community level. It also enables local languages and dialects to be heard, valued and celebrated, encouraging pride and creativity in the learners' history and their future.

Conclusion: critical approaches to teaching literacies

Freire (1993) argued that critical educational practice is not a specific methodology to be applied without insight but rather one that emerges when tutors can practise teaching from a critical perspective and have the time to reflect on their pedagogy. As busy practitioners finding the time for reflection can be difficult. However, it is vital to try and find this space in your working day to ensure you maintain your autonomy and

Name		Tutor	
Date		Class	

Daily Job Sheet

James keeps a record of the time he has spent working on the various jobs during his working day. The document is used to calculate his pay and the customer's bill, therefore it must always be an honest and accurate account of time spent.

Here is a sample daily job sheet:

TECHNICIAN'S DAILY JOB SHEET

NAME: James Miller					CLOCK NO: 001621		DATE: Fri 21 Sept.	
Job Number	Code Number	Schedule Time	Actual Time	Time Gained	Time Lost	Date/Authorised		Clocking: ON/OFF
PT09251	A12500	1:0.0	1:4.5	0:0.0	0:1.5	21/9	SS	9.00 / 10.45
PT09260	A6000	1:0.0	1:2.5	0:0.5	0:0.0	21/9	SS	10.50 / 12.15
PT09265	B0010	2:00	2:20	0:00	0:00	21/9	SS	12.45 / 14.45
TOTAL						BONUS		
BROUGHT FORWARD FROM PREVIOUS SHEET		28:00	28:30	0:15	0:45	OVERTIME		
WEEKLY TOTAL						AUTHORISED		

James's final job of the day, job number PT09273 is a 20,000 mile service, code number A20000. James begins the job at 15:00 hours. It is scheduled to take 2 hours but he completes the work in 2 hours 10 minutes (time lost 10 minutes).

Fill in James's daily job sheet for him. Complete the sections marked in yellow.

Source: reproduced with permission from Gatehouse Books (2009)

Figure 4.3   Daily job sheet

professional integrity. When reflecting you may want to consider how many noncritical curriculums may have the potential to move towards a critical pedagogy. It is a good idea to avoid categorizing curriculums and practice as either critical or noncritical, but think of them as a continuum between noncritical and critical. An example of this is when tutors may have to use a pre-written curriculum but may also implement a more reflective and critical pedagogy that empower learners. Such tutors may be viewed as shaping their pedagogy from noncritical to critical. The changes can be small or big but it is not about everything or nothing; it is about reflection and identifying spaces within the curriculum to facilitate both you and your learners to be thoughtful and take agency, rather than being respectively passive deliverers and recipients of knowledge.

Literacy teaching can be delivered as a transformative model otherwise known as 'critical literacy'. Taking a 'critical reflection' approach to literacy means being responsive to individual and community needs. It means encouraging learners to look beyond 'reading the word' to 'reading the world', and becoming actors in developing their own communities and societies (Freire, 1993).

References

Barton, D. (1994) *Literacy: An Introduction to the Ecology of Written Language*. Oxford: Blackwell.

Barton, D. and Hamilton, M. (1998) *Local Literacies: Reading and Writing in One Community*. London: Routledge.

Barton, D., Ivanic, R., Appleby, Y., Hodge, R. and Tusting, K. (2007) *Literacy, Lives and Learning*. London: Routledge.

Bynner, J. and Parsons, S. (2006) *New Light on Literacy and Numeracy*. London: National Research and Development Centre (NRDC).

Casey, H., Cara, O., Eldred, J., Grief, S., Hodge, R., Ivanic, R., Jupp, T., Lopez, D. and McNeil, B. (2006) *You Wouldn't Expect a Maths Teacher to Teach Plastering. Embedding Literacy, Language and Numeracy in Post-16 Vocational Programmes: The Impact on Learning and Achievement*. London: National Resource and Development Centre (NRDC).

Department for Education and Skills (DfES) (1999) *A Fresh Start: Improving Literacy and Numeracy*. Available online at www.dfes.gov.uk/afreshstart

Department for Education and Skills (DfES) (2001) *Skills for Life*. Available online at www.dfes.gov.uk/skillsforlife

Department for Education and Skills (DfES) (2003) *21st Century Skills: Realising our Potential*. Available online at www.dfes.gov.uk/skillsstrategy

Dolan, M. (2008) *Write About . . . Bullying*. Warrington: Gatehouse Books.

Duckworth, V. (2008) *Getting Better Worksheets*. Warrington: Gatehouse Books.

Freire, P. (1993) *Pedagogy of the Oppressed*. New York: Continuum.

Gatehouse Books (2009) *On The Job: Car Mechanic*. Warrington: Gatehouse Books.

Gee, J. (1996) *Social Linguistics and Literacies: Ideology in Discourses*, 2nd edn. London: RoutledgeFalmer.

HM Treasury (2006) *The Leitch Report: Prosperity for All in the Global Economy – World Class Skills*. London: HM Treasury.

Hunt, J. et al. (2005) *E-learning, Skills for Life and Teacher Training,* Reflect (4). Available online at www.nrdc.org.uk/content.asp?categoryID=1029

Ivanic, R. et al. (2008) Harnessing everyday literacies for student learning at college, *Teaching and Learning Research Briefing*, No. 50. Available online at www.hrp.org/publdocuments/IvanicRB50final.pdf

Lifelong Learning UK (LLUK) (2006) *New Overarching Professional Standards for Teachers, Tutors and Trainers in the Lifelong Learning Sector*. London: LLUK.

Long, R. (2005) *Motivation*. London: David Fulton.

McNamara, M. (2007) *Getting Better.* Warrington: Gatehouse Books.

Mellar, H., Kambouri, M., Logan, K., Betts, S., Nance, B. and Moriarty, V. (2007) *Effective Teaching and Learning Using ICT.* London: National Research and Development Centre (NRDC).

Street, B. (1984) *Literacy in Theory and Practice*. Cambridge: Cambridge University Press.

The Polling Report (2004) Available online at www.edition.cnn.com/election/2004/pages/results/electoral.college/ (accessed 12 November 2009).

5   The employability agenda

The objectives of this chapter

This chapter provides an overview and rationale of the employability agenda. It looks at conceptualizing employability, entrepreneurship and enterprise as transferable skills. To support this it explores embedding employability, entrepreneurship and enterprise across diverse curricular contexts.

This chapter addresses the following professional practice standards for Qualified Teacher Learning and Skills (QTLS):

BK 2.2   Ways to engage, motivate and encourage active participation of learners and learner independence.

BK 2.5   Ways of using learners' own experience as a foundation for learning.

FK 3.1   Progression and career opportunities within own specialist area.

FK 4.2   Processes for liaison with colleagues and other professionals to provide effective guidance and support for learners.

(LLUK, 2006)

Introduction: an overview and rationale of the employability agenda

Over 10 years ago, *The Learning Age* document supported Britain's drive for business and commerce, noting that: 'Learning will be the key to a strong economy and an inclusive society' (DfEE, 1998: 3). Four years later, another key government policy document, *Success for All*, stated how the government's goals should be 'social inclusion and economic prosperity' (DfES, 2002: 9). The rhetoric being used in the policies and reports correspond to an instrumental model with a drive towards employability in the labour market as the key to social inclusion. With this in mind, employability has acquired a central role within policy, strategy and the student curriculum in the lifelong learning sector (LLS).

Globalization, competition and rapid progress of technology have caused a shift in the nature and patterns of working life and employment. Current plans for the UK are ambitious: in 2010, the UK commission stated:

> It is our ambition to be one of the top countries in the world – for jobs, for productivity and for skills. A World Class economy, built on World Class skills, supporting World Class jobs and businesses. We should aim to be in the top quartile of OECD countries in all three – jobs, productivity and skills – by 2020. This means being in the top eight countries of the world. Our future prosperity depends ultimately on employment and productivity: how many people are in work and how productive they are when they are in work. Skills are essential to both. If we are to become World Class, we must raise our game to match the productivity, skills and jobs of the best.
>
> (DfES, 2002: 6)

Today, due to shifts in working patterns of employment, people do not have the same stability of employment or the same length of service with a single employer. The concept of a 'job for life' now seems a thing of the past to many people. Consider your own history: many of your parents and perhaps grandparents would have held down the same job, or would have progressed 'through the ranks' within a single firm or company through the course of their working lives. Many of them might have received a clock, ornament or certificate on retiring as a reminder and token of the years they had spent working for the same employer. By contrast, many working people have been displaced from traditional to new forms of work. A good example of this is in the implementation of information and communication technology (ICT) across many industrial sectors. In many workplaces, previously labour-intensive processes have been automated, with ICT changing the nature of work, speed and volume of communication, information and working practices. We live in what is frequently referred to by politicians and economists as a 'knowledge economy'. In 2008, a report by the Teaching and Learning Research Briefing identified how the

> demand for knowledge workers rises exponentially in the knowledge economy [and] has resulted in a shift from mechanical Taylorism to digital Taylorism, so that knowledge work becomes portable working knowledge
>
> (Ivanic et al., 2008: 1)

'Taylorism', named after the late-nineteenth-century industrialist Frederick Taylor, is a term used to refer to a particular kind of theory of management that aims to improve labour productivity.

One of the most significant duties given to education is to provide a flexible, adaptable and skilled workforce to make countries competitive in the globalized economy. In other words, the purpose of education, according to this political and economic perspective, is to prepare people for the world of work, rather than, for example, to encourage learning for learning's sake, or to encourage education as a means to generate a particular kind of civilized society. A focus on education for work positions education as a commodity, and pays no regard to issues of economic, political and social equality. For example, learners from socio-economically deprived areas may not have the same access to opportunities as those who live in more affluent areas who would be better able to attend high-achieving state schools or receive a private education. Thus, school success may be seen as linked by 'the amount and type of cultural capital inherited from the family milieu rather than by measures of individual talent or achievement' (Reay et al., 2005: 19). For the children who face such structural inequalities, the choices they have on leaving school or college can be limited and can impact on their life chances, such as opportunities for future education, training and future employment. Many learners who leave school without qualifications face the prospect of unemployment, or entering low-paid unskilled jobs. However, there are a number of incentives aimed at re-engaging those young people who are deemed to be at risk, and motivating them to stay in learning, such as the Education Maintenance Allowance (EMA).

The EMA is a financial incentive aimed at 16-, 17- and 18-year-olds to encourage them to stay in further education (FE). Payments of between £10–30 a week, depending on household income, are made directly to those young people on a course at an FE college, on an apprenticeship or on an Entry to Employment (E2E) programme. Further bonus payments are made to learners who are seen as making good progress and 'doing well' on their course or learning programme; measuring such progress can vary between institutions, but tends to revolve around attendance and achievement. The EMA is promoted on the back of statistics relating to educational achievement and employability – nor can there be any doubt relating to the desirability of keeping young people in education and training:

> In the UK evaluation evidence shows that Education Maintenance Allowances (EMA) have resulted in staying-on rates in full-time education that are higher than would otherwise have occurred. The initiative also appears to have positive impacts on parental attitudes to staying-on among young people.
>
> (McQuaid et al., 2010: 16)

However, we should not focus solely on young people. Re-entering education later in life, through the LLS, is a means for older learners to gain new skills to aid reintegration into the labour market, perhaps after redundancy or time spent managing family affairs. However, this sense of reintegration is not without problems: those learners who may have been made redundant and need to retrain for a second career or job in middle age can experience anxiety as pressure is placed on them to reinvent themselves. The pressure to develop new skills and fit into a new career is not an easy option for many learners. And there are also a number of incentives and schemes aimed at older workers, who need to upskill or reskill, such as Train to Gain, which was introduced in 2006 to provide subsidized training to allow unqualified employees to gain qualifications at Level 2 of the National Qualifications Framework (NQF), bringing benefits to both the employee and the employer.

The idea of employability

The opportunities offered for adults by FE colleges, adult education centres and local education authorities (LEAs) can at one level, therefore, be seen as being all about employability: encouraging it, developing it and helping learners recognize the need to enhance it. But how should we define it?

Employability may be approached at an individual level: a person having the skills, knowledge, attitudes and behaviours required to look for, gain and maintain employment in the labour market can be seen as employable. In this sense, employability is positioned as an individual characteristic. The onus is on the individual to take responsibility for further training for – in effect – their economic and social well-being; it is not the direct responsibility of the state.

Task: enhancing employability awareness

Consider the teaching or training that you do in your specialist subject area. In what ways do the qualifications that your learners receive prepare them for employment? Are they directly linked to a particular trade or profession? Do they act as a gateway to further training that will then lead to employment? Or do they aim to provide learners with a more generic set of skills that will help them gain employment at a later date?

Embedding employability

Establishing links between curricula and employability are at first glance quite straightforward. A consideration of such issues can help us, as teachers and trainers, to develop a greater understanding of the profiles of our learners, in terms of both needs and motivation. At a straightforward level, we can see that for many learners, their choice of course reflects a choice of career. But this is not always the case. For example, Jackie has taught beauty therapy at a mixed FE college for five years. Most of her teaching is at the college's main site in the middle of the city. But she also teaches a class in an outreach centre, attached to a secondary school in a large housing estate. In the following case study, Jackie reflects on the differences between two student groups, one in each of these two locations, and their prospects after finishing their level two courses.

Case study: reflecting on the progress of beauty therapy learners

Nearly the end of the year! There are just a couple of teaching weeks left, but all the portfolios have been sent to the external verifier now. These last sessions are for advice and guidance. I am pretty sure that I will see a fair few of the girls again next year for the level three, but some won't come back. Most of the college girls will return: they are all quite keen to work, and some of them have even got work experience or Saturday jobs in salons already. A couple were talking about setting up their own businesses, but they just need to get their level three and then do a business course as well if they want to do that. Running a salon is really hard! The college group seem to have the most realistic sense of the kind of work they could get, and why they need to come back rather than trying to find work with just a level two qualification.

The thing I found hardest was talking to the community education group about next year, or about what they might do next. They seem really unrealistic about the kinds or amount of work available, but mostly don't want to commit to another year. Really, I don't think that they want to work in the industry at all. But they didn't seem keen to come back or maybe transfer to a different course. I guess things like customer skills are useful things to get from the course, but I don't know how far that will help them if they want to go back to work.

So what is the relationship between this Level 2 course in beauty therapy and employability? Clearly, it is too simplistic to suggest that beauty therapy students all go on to become beauty therapists. So if this course, or any other, is to be seen as providing 'building blocks' towards employability, then there must be some component within it that serves to do so, in just the same way that there are components within such courses that help learners to develop their literacy and numeracy skills. So, is 'employability' a subject in its own right, or is it somehow embedded within other subjects?

An employability curriculum

Employability, together with enterprise and entrepreneurship, are now seen as essential features in qualification development. This may be viewed as an approach to, and a context for, learning that aims to encourage good teaching practice and makes links with the world of employment. Many of the curricula that are now being delivered, implemented and evaluated will have employment at the heart of their design. As such, employability skills are part of the planning process for a range of programmes including 14–19 Diplomas, Foundation Learning and Apprenticeship provision. The five key area of the core curriculum are:

1 communication
2 numeracy
3 ICT
4 problem solving
5 working with others.

The skills listed above are deemed necessary for entrants to the job market to-day. And so, the integration of these skills into the curriculum, which can be seen as enhancing employability, can enable modules, themes and assignments to be made relevant to the LLS, graduate labour market and professional training routes. But can 'employability skills' be taught in their own right?

In the following case study, Danielle Vipond, a trainee teacher and specialist in business studies, shares her experience of delivering employability skills training.

Case study: gaining employability skills alongside another qualification

The BTEC Level 2 qualifications in employability skills enable the students alongside their normal course to learn practical skills that will make them more employable. The course is an innovative training programme which balances practical skills with aspects of personal and social skills. The students gain an understanding of what it is like when they move into the work place, giving them a taste of being managed, presenting and working as teams. The course also gives them an understanding of real life situations. I did a lesson on diversity, where the students learned about not judging people by stereotyping. When going into the workplace students will come across all different types of people and learning to understand not to take people at face value is a very good skill. Having a background in business myself enables me to use real life experiences when teaching the subject. The students get to relate theory to life experiences. I like to encourage the students to get more involved in what happens in the work place, for example learning about employment law and what trade unions are gives them a better understanding of things that happen in the news (the students used the example of Royal Mail for trade unions).

From my own experiences of going to university and straight into a job, there were areas of work you do not get told about, even simple things like having a good CV is not taught as a necessary subject. The students on the course are part of the finance career academy, a two-year course, which has special business led lectures, seminars and company visits. Each student is given a mentor from the local business community and a six-week paid internship with a major employer during the summer. Not only does this give the students the opportunity of being in a workplace, it gives them first-hand experience in using the skills they have developed. Both the employability skills and the academy help the students get to learn how to network with business people, which is normally a skill we only learn when we are in the workplace, but is a very important tool in the business world, and getting connections before starting in the work place can help a lot of students find a job. This kind of course seems to be growing within the post-compulsory sector, as employers are needing employees to have these kind of key skills (it reduces the cost of training) and creating a better work force improves not only the economy, but also gives students who may not necessary want a academic route (in order to go on to university) a place to study something that they feel will get them a better job.

Danielle raises a number of key issues here related to employability skills specifically, but also to the broader notion of preparing students for the workplace. These issues are worth unpacking in a little more detail.

Bringing the world of work into the classroom

One example of how, as tutors or trainers, we can embed employability into our vocational areas is to use case studies based on the learning journeys of former students. We might want to consider the aims and aspirations of role models such as these and how we can link these into a discussion with your own learners. Below is an extract taken from the story of James, a young student who wanted to become a car mechanic. An interest in cars acted as a motivation for him to gain those qualifications that he would need in order to undertake his mechanic's training:

> As a kid, I'd always been interested in cars and how they work and I really wanted to learn a bit more about them and get into the trade. I got my GCSEs at school – I had to have Maths and English at grade C or above – then I got my qualifications through college and my apprenticeship.
>
> (Duckworth, 2009: 6)

As well as telling stories about past learners, tutors can then design or use resources that in some way capture or draw on these same stories. So, returning to James, tutors could then use resources such as these in their classrooms or workshops (see Figs. 5.1–5.3).

And there are many other ways by which the real world of work can be brought inside educational settings, some of which are relatively commonplace while others are more unusual.

Hair and beauty salons

Many FE colleges have hair and beauty salons that are used by trainees. These are usually open to the public as well. It is important to note that they provide learning experiences that are not only related to the profession (i.e. hairdressing or beauty therapy) but are also related to the management of a business in the sector. Using computer systems to book appointments, taking payments and reconciling a cash register are three examples of the kinds of transferable employment skill that can be practised.

Training restaurants and kitchens

Catering colleges often have restaurants that are open to the public as well as to staff and students, and that cater for large events such as Christmas dinners, as well as small private bookings. As with hair and beauty salons, there are also opportunities for learning more generic business skills.

Cabin crew training

A small number of colleges that offer training for cabin crew staff have gone to tremendous lengths to recreate a realistic working environment by purchasing decommissioned aeroplanes for trainees to work in. One of the authors of this book (Jonathan)

Name		Tutor	
Date		Class	

Wordsearch

Find the hidden words in the grid.

Words can go across, up, down and in two diagonals.

```
n  t  r  x  o  i  l  h  n  k  l  n  j  t  h  n  n  q
e  q  e  n  m  l  h  f  m  k  t  f  n  n  d  o  f  h
g  n  a  x  v  n  l  i  e  n  y  o  b  v  i  i  n  y
a  l  r  z  l  t  l  l  k  n  r  d  e  e  e  s  n  n
e  v  m  r  f  w  r  t  a  f  r  v  s  i  s  s  j  z
l  e  n  g  i  n  e  e  r  h  i  i  d  n  e  i  t  h
i  h  k  d  d  s  x  r  b  r  o  g  i  d  l  m  g  m
m  i  n  p  a  n  t  c  d  n  y  e  u  i  p  s  x  t
e  c  e  k  e  s  h  e  r  b  r  m  l  c  r  n  n  k
c  l  t  x  c  t  h  m  e  y  b  l  f  a  j  a  m  w
n  e  w  d  h  q  r  b  t  r  f  z  l  t  l  r  e  k
a  y  z  t  r  a  h  o  o  p  i  w  m  o  q  t  c  r
t  l  q  l  m  x  u  l  l  a  c  n  o  r  n  l  i  w
s  b  i  r  p  f  e  s  q  c  r  c  g  f  m  d  v  h
i  z  d  g  k  e  t  j  t  g  l  d  q  p  r  r  r  g
d  m  t  r  h  h  e  a  d  l  a  m  p  c  d  l  e  q
n  d  p  w  t  t  b  c  o  r  r  o  s  i  o  n  s  p
z  r  m  y  t  v  c  t  t  e  c  h  n  i  c  i  a  n
```

brake	coolant	corrosion	dashboard	diesel	distance
drive	engine	exhaust	filter	fluid	front
headlamp	indicator	light	mileage	noise	oil
petrol	rear	service	steering	technician	transmission
tyre	vehicle	wheel			

Source: reproduced with permission from Gatehouse Books (2009)

Figure 5.1 On the job: car mechanic tutor resources

worked at a college where the cabin crew course team had bought an aeroplane. On one occasion, he expressed surprise to one of his PGCE students, who taught the cabin crew trainees, that such a large piece of kit had been purchased. Her response, accompanied by a look of disbelief, was: 'how else do you think we can train the students properly? How can we prepare stewards and stewardesses for work if they've never been assessed in a plane, even if it's only on the ground?'

Name		Tutor	
Date		Class	

Looking for a Job

Here are 2 job advertisements. In order to do the following task, you can use the above examples or find your own.

Company: Makerson Accident & Repair Service

Panel Beater, Car Bodyshop, Manchester, competitive rate + bonus.
About the role: We are currently seeking to recruit a Panel Beater to repair and replace the panels of accident-damaged vehicles in line with manufacturer's specifications.
About you: You will ideally have served a recognised apprenticeship and gained a technical qualification, although individuals who have trained on-the-job will also be considered. Either way, you must have previous experience of working in a busy bodyshop and be willing to work shifts and weekends. **Contract:** Full Time.

Company: Repairers and Restorers

The ideal candidate will be: Fully Qualified Post Apprenticeship at 2 years post qualified. A working knowledge of Motor Mechanics. WE ARE THE PREMIER AUTOMOTIVE RECRUITMENT AGENCY FOR MOTOR TRADE. Automotive Main Car Dealerships such as Mercedes, Audi, BMW, VW, Jaguar, Land Rover, Volvo, Bentley, Saab, Lexus, Toyota. **Contract:** Full Time **Salary:** £15,000 to £17,500

Find your own job

To find your own job advertisements, you may want to look through the local/ national newspapers, visit websites, ask friends or visit your local job centre or library. Make a note of the details of the job below:

Company:
About the role:

Qualifications & Skills Required:

Source: reproduced with permission from Gatehouse Books (2009)

Figure 5.2 On the job: car mechanic tutor resources

| Name | _____ | Tutor | _____ |
| Date | _____ | Class | _____ |

Writing a Covering Letter

Write a letter to apply for a job of your choice. Here is some help, if you need it.

Write your name and address below:

_____

_____

_____

_____

Write the date on the line: _____

Petersfield Motors
London Road
Basingstoke
DT227AG

Dear Sir or Madam

I am writing to apply for the position of   _____

_____

_____

_____

Yours faithfully

Now sign your name

Source: reproduced with permission from Gatehouse Books (2009)

Figure 5.3   On the job: car mechanic tutor resources

Employability: more than transferable skills

Thus far, we have considered employability in terms of individual, discrete skills that are transferable across contexts. In other words, if as a consequence of taking part in an education or training programme, an individual possesses skills such as problem solving or numeracy, then they are said to be 'employable'. There is a lot more to it than this, of course, but the theory is coherent enough: employability skills are in some way possessed by an individual who can add to them throughout life (by doing further training or by learning on the job) and carry them from workplace to workplace like a toolkit.

So far so good. But the problem with an analysis such as this is that it fails to take account of where our recently qualified student is actually taking all these skills. Obviously, for many occupations, quite specific qualifications are necessary. Becoming a midwife requires more than just a range of generic qualifications and good results in key skills tests: it requires specific qualifications and experience. A student on a business studies course might consider a range of possible employment options on completion of their studies. But going to work for a credit card insurance company in a call centre will surely require quite different skills from going to work as an office junior for a high street firm of solicitors. The point is that employability is also somehow connected to the kinds of working environment that people find themselves in. It is all well and good for government departments and SSCs to talk about employability and to want education and training providers to do more to make students employable. But surely these employability skills need in some way to match up to, to be in alignment with, a workplace?

The answer (if there is one) probably lies somewhere between. Clearly, specific working environments have particular practices and procedures, and require particular knowledge and expertise, and people who work there will have to acquire or obtain or get used to all these factors. At the same time, it seems somehow right, even if only at a commonsense level, to say that there must be particular skills or competencies that college courses or community education programmes can help students acquire that will help them not only get the job in the first place, but also go about working out just what those practices and procedures actually are.

So far we have considered a number of factors relating to employability skills. We have looked at the notion of discrete and transferable employability skills, and we have considered how they might be delivered on a standalone basis, or on an embedded basis. And we have thought about the ways in which employability skills depend on or respond to different workplace environments. A further way in which employability has been researched relates to gender, and we turn to this theme next.

Research focus: men and women's attitudes to employability training

'An analysis of gendered attitudes and responses to employability training', a research paper, written by John Willott and Jacqueline Stevenson from Leeds Metropolitan University, was published in 2006. The article was based on research that had been carried out relating to training courses for a range of 'at-risk' adults, including people who were unemployed, people with mental health difficulties and people who were vulnerably housed. It sought to explore how the participants in employability training courses defined the barriers to employment that they encountered. These barriers were defined in three ways:

1   Practical barriers: examples included access to affordable child care or to public transport links.
2   Academic barriers: examples included both the lack of qualifications and specific learning difficulties such as dyslexia.
3   Personal barriers: examples included feelings of low self-esteem, poor motivation and low levels of confidence.

Barriers to employment such as these are strikingly similar to the kinds of barrier to learning that are frequently referred to within the teacher-training literature. But the interesting theme that Willott and Stevenson (2006) identified was that the women they interviewed tended to cite personal barriers as the prime factor in wanting to improve their employability skills, whereas the men tended to cite practical barriers. Interestingly, both groups focused more on the need to gain skills and experience rather than the need to obtain actual qualifications.

So where does research such as this lead us? Perhaps a further way by which employability can be enhanced is not only through the development of key or hard skills, but also through soft skills such as motivation and confidence. In this sense, employability is something that could, arguably, be enhanced by any form of education or training that helps to improve participants' self-esteem. And the development of self-esteem, as well as those other characteristics that we have discussed here, are commonly cited as being important outcomes of many kinds of adult education programme, not just those that are solely linked to the vocational curriculum.

Higher education and employability

The employability agenda is not restricted to the further and adult education sectors, however. Increasingly, higher education institutions (HEIs) are tailoring their curricula in response to concerns that graduates lack the generic skills that employers need. And since FE colleges are increasingly involved in the delivery of HE programmes, many tutors working within them will need to be aware of how the employability agenda impacts on those courses. Extension courses, foundation degrees, franchised courses and top-up degrees are increasingly common, and for many students, studying at a local FE college is preferable to travelling to a more distant university. In fact, the scale of what is generally known as HE in FE provision is considerable:

- over 10 per cent of all HE provision is delivered in FE colleges
- over 30 per cent of all students in FE colleges are following degree-level programmes
- over 70 per cent of FE colleges deliver HE programmes

So how does the HE sector define employability skills?

> Employability' refers to a graduate's achievements and his/her potential to obtain a 'graduate job', and should not be confused with the actual acquisition of a 'graduate job' (which is subject to influences in the environment, a major influence being the state of the economy). Employability derives from complex learning, and is a concept of wider range than those of 'core' and 'key' skills.
>
> (Yorke, 2008: 3)

Clearly, to ensure that issues of employability are being clearly addressed, universities need to be embedding employability into their curricula to improve graduates' opportunities in the labour market. Ways to do this include:

- embedding higher level key skills in the academic curricula
- increasing and enhancing opportunities for work-related learning
- preparing for work in a global economy
- delivering effective careers education, information and guidance
- recording academic achievement and personal development.

Conclusion

So what is employability and how does the LLS help to develop it? One widely established definition of employability rests on three themes:

- the ability to gain initial employment
- the ability to maintain employment
- the ability to obtain new employment if required.

And the LLS can be said to contribute to the employability agenda in a number of ways:

- through providing courses that allow employability skills to develop alongside the curriculum
- through specialist provision (such as E2E) that specifically addressed the skills that young people need to find work
- through specialist courses that deliver employability according to a key skills model.

Developing employability skills may be considered important in sustaining a competitive advantage in a global economy based on innovation and enterprise. Having the opportunity to identify and nurture employment potential among young and older learners can have positive long-term implications for the UK's economic development. Employability education can be an intervention strategy for students in at-risk and urban environments plagued by structural disadvantages of social and economic disparities. To address this further, disparity and work towards a more inclusive approach to employability, the relationship between school and society needs to be further addressed and critically explored in policies of the intermeshing of local, national and global developments that so powerfully influence growing up and working in today's society.

References

Department for Education and Employment (DfEE) (1998) *The Learning Age*. London: DfEE.

Department for Education and Skills (DfES) (2002) *Success for All*. London: DfES.

Duckworth, V. (2009) *On The Job: Car Mechanic*. Warrington: Gatehouse Books.

Ivanic, R. et al. (2008) Harnessing everyday literacies for student learning at college, *Teaching and Learning and Research Briefing*, No. 50. Available online at www./lrp.org/pub/document/IvanichRB50final.pdf

Lifelong Learning UK (LLUK) (2006) *New Overarching Professional Standards for Teachers, Tutors and Trainers in the Lifelong Learning Sector*. London: LLUK.

McQuaid, R., Lindsay, C. and Johnson, S. (2010) *An Appetite for Learning: Increasing Employee Demands for Skills Development*. London: UK Commission for Employment and Skills.

Reay, D., David, M.E. and Ball, S. (2005) *Degrees of Choice: Social Class, Race and Gender in Higher Education*. Stoke-on-Trent: Trentham Books.

UK Commission for Employment and Skills (UKCES) (2009) *Ambition 2020: World Class Skills and Jobs for the UK*. London: UKCES.

Willott, J. and Stevenson, J. (2006) An analysis of gendered attitudes and responses to employability training, *Journal of Vocational Education and Training*, 58(4): 441–53.

Yorke, M. (2008) *Employability in Higher Education: What It Is – What It Is Not*, 2nd edn. York: Higher Education Academy.

6 Exploring the curriculum in the lifelong learning sector

Chapter objectives

This chapter looks at the curriculum in the lifelong learning sector (LLS). After offering ways of defining curriculum, it goes on to consider examples of recent changes to provision in the sector, together with an exploration of the governmental agendas that underpin such changes.

Professional standards

This chapter addresses the following professional practice standards for Qualified Teacher Learning and Skills (QTLS):

AK 2.2   **Ways in which learning promotes the emotional, intellectual, social and economic well-being of individuals and the population as a whole.**

DP1.1   **Plan coherent and inclusive learning programmes that meet learners' needs and curriculum requirements, promote equality and engage with diversity effectively.**

(LLUK, 2006)

Introduction

'Curriculum' is a difficult word to pin down. This might be seen as a distinct disadvantage when reading a chapter entitled 'exploring the curriculum in the lifelong learning sector'. But it is the 'exploring' part that helps us, as teachers and trainers, to make sense of all the contexts in which the word 'curriculum' gets used. Sometimes it is used to define a subject or a topic: 'the motor vehicle curriculum' or 'the hair and beauty' curriculum, for example. At other times, it is used when describing a broader area of study and work: 'the vocational curriculum' or 'the adult numeracy core curriculum'. When prefixed with a variety of other terms, educationalists and sociologists use the word 'curriculum' to analyse particular effects or consequences of educational provision. 'The hidden curriculum' and 'the total curriculum' are examples of this. It can also be used to describe the different ways in which an educational programme can be organized, delivered as a 'spiral curriculum' or a 'thematic curriculum'. Put simply, it is a word that does a lot of work, and that requires careful consideration of the context within which it is found. But once these contexts and meanings are established, an understanding of curriculum studies, an exploration of curriculum, can be extremely fruitful in providing us with insights into not only why courses or programmes of study are planned, delivered and assessed in the ways that they are, but also why they are offered in the first place, what happens to the students who travel through them, and how current political as well as educational debates shape the curricula that are found in the LLS.

A single chapter such as this is not really sufficient to do justice to the kinds of term mentioned above: concepts such as the hidden curriculum are complex and nuanced, and deserve much lengthier exploration. To that end, references to a number of more specialized texts appear at the end of this chapter. But for now, we briefly note those definitions of curriculum that impact on the more specific contemporary political and educational debates that follow.

Defining terms: theories and models of curriculum

Briefly, then, we might expect to find curriculum discussed in the following ways:

1   The total curriculum and the hidden curriculum
2   The planned curriculum and the received curriculum
3   Curriculum as process and product
4   Spiral, thematic and linear curricula.

We look at these in turn.

1 The total curriculum and the hidden curriculum

The total curriculum is a useful concept that allows us to move beyond merely equating 'curriculum' with 'syllabus' (which is what most commonplace definitions tend to do, and which is how curriculum initially tends to be discussed by teacher-training students). An understanding of the total curriculum takes us beyond the subjects or topics being taught, to consider broader issues to do with why the curriculum is being offered in the first place and what the implications are for all those involved: students, tutors and other stakeholders such as employers and funding bodies.

The hidden curriculum, by contrast, refers to all those aspects or consequences of a curriculum that are normally left unspoken by policy makers, tutors, students and stakeholders. There are two themes at work here. First, there are those elements that are hidden from those people for whom the curriculum is intended: that is, the students. Second, there are those elements that are hidden from those people who are involved in establishing and delivering the curriculum: tutors, college managers and employers.

Examples of such elements are issues around access (does the time and place at which a course is offered serve to restrict access to it?), or issues relating to gender or race (is the gender or racial profile of a group of students on a particular course representative of the gender or racial profile of the college or region as a whole?).

2 The planned curriculum and the received curriculum

How a curriculum is to be delivered (i.e. taught, assessed and evaluated) can be said to constitute the planned curriculum. Put simply, the planned curriculum is the 'official version' of a course or programme of study, and would typically include content, outcomes, resources, assessment strategies and evaluation procedures. And so awarding bodies and examination boards such as City and Guilds or Open College produce (at times considerable) quantities of documents that set out, in varying degrees of detail, how courses should be run. Adherence to the guidance set out in course handbooks and syllabuses is commonly a feature of the quality assurance processes established by awarding bodies to which providers have to adhere. And so external verifiers or moderators will inspect college-based provision on a regular basis to make sure the course is being delivered 'correctly'.

But the reality of the workshop or seminar room is some way removed from the course documentation sent out by awarding bodies. It surely cannot be much of a surprise for us to learn that not only do some students enjoy some parts of a course more than others, but also that some tutors enjoy teaching some parts of a course more than others. Nor are the subjective likes and dislikes of tutors and students the only variable. Many other factors can have an impact on how a curriculum is actually delivered: the time of day at which it is timetabled; the quality of the teaching accommodation; the quality and sufficiency of resources; and the expertise of the tutor. These are just some of the things that can have an impact on the received curriculum: the curriculum as it is actually experienced by students and staff.

3 Curriculum as process and product

Process and product models of curriculum refer to the perceived goals of a curriculum, and imply particular views of learning as well. A product model of curriculum (also known as an objectives model) implies a sole focus on the observable outcomes of the curriculum: what can a student actually do after completing a course or programme of study? Product models rest on specific observable outcomes and as such imply a behaviourist or neo-behaviourist approach to learning. Process models, by contrast, place a greater emphasis on what happens to the student and what the student experiences during a course. This is not to deny the importance of certification or any other warrant of successful completion. But the activity of learning, of learning how to learn, is as important as the stuff that will be covered during the course. As such, a process curriculum can be seen as resting on cognitive models of learning, with tutors acting in a facilitative role.

4 Spiral, thematic and linear curricula

The ways in which curricula are organized, or sequenced, can essentially be classified in one of three ways. In a linear curriculum, each topic is taught and then assessed in turn, and then put to one side; that is, there is no formal pedagogic need for the student to revisit that work. A spiral curriculum, in contrast, is structured so that the student will indeed revisit topics or themes throughout the programme of study, exploring those themes at greater levels of complexity each time. In a thematic curriculum, key themes, posited as being central to the entire course, are embedded throughout the programme as a whole; that is, such themes are taught, studied and assessed at all stages of the course.

A cautionary note

It is important to note that these concepts are not the only ways in which we can talk about curriculum, but they are the most common. Similarly, it is important to remember that the concepts discussed here are not mutually exclusive: it is quite feasible, for example, to describe a curriculum as having both linear and spiral elements. Thinking that a particular curriculum has significant hidden components does not prevent us from also thinking about the ways in which it might be both planned and received. Concepts such as these are not intended to act merely as labels or convenient definitions, but to help us explore the curricula with which we work.

Task: theorizing our own curricula

Before reading on, take some time to think about how these models and concepts might be applied to curricula with which you are familiar. If you are already working as a teacher or trainer, while studying part time for your QTLS award, you may well be involved in teaching multiple curricula, perhaps set by different awarding bodies and in different subjects. If you are a full-time teacher-training student, your experiences might be more marginal, depending on the kind of teaching that you have done, or are going to do, while on placement. If this is the case, talk to your mentor about one of the curricula that they are engaged with in order to develop your own knowledge and understanding. Which of the concepts described above (process/product, linear/spiral, etc.) help to unpack the curriculum in question? What is the nature of the hidden curriculum? How might the curriculum as it is planned be different from how it is experienced by the students?

Changing and shaping curricula

It can be said that ideas about 'learning for learning's sake' persist through the perpetuation of a 'canon' of knowledge that young people ought to be exposed to. Arguments about whether or not schoolchildren should study Shakespeare, or whether learning a second language should be a compulsory part of the national curriculum, are good examples of this. More often in contemporary times, however, the things that should be included within a curriculum are shaped by quite different agendas. These include, among others, the perceived needs of the UK economy; the specific requirements of particular industrial or commercial sectors; and the skills for life agenda. The LLS is particularly prone to rapid and continuous change. Shifting political targets, combined with redistributed public funds, have resulted in an at times bewildering array of initiatives, targets and new curricular agendas, both the scale and speed of which have, arguably, increased since 1997. The impact of such a rapid pace of change on the LLS workforce can be profound. While the casualization of the workforce that was characteristic of further and adult education in the years immediately following the incorporation of further education (FE) colleges has now subsided (partly, perhaps, thanks to the reprofessionalization of the workforce as described in Chapter 1), professional uncertainties, relating to job role as well as to security, persist. It is not uncommon for tutors to find themselves being asked to teach subject areas that they are unfamiliar with to student groups that they have not worked with before. Changes to funding can lead to whole areas of the curriculum being reduced in scope, with class numbers cut and, consequently, tutor numbers reduced. Some areas of provision, for example, adult literacy, numeracy and English for speakers of other languages (ESOL), would appear to be particularly prone to such change.

Other areas of what might be termed the 'vocational curriculum', such as hairdressing or electrical engineering, can perhaps be characterized as more prone to change as a consequence of employer influence, most conspicuously through Sector Skills Councils (SSCs). Here, a slightly different imperative can be distinguished. Notwithstanding an overall sense of curriculum provision being driven by some kind of economic, business or employment agenda (which alongside softer if somewhat more nebulous concepts such as 'life skills' embodies the contemporary dominating discourses that shape the LLS), it is surely both appropriate and understandable for specific industries, or other sectors of the economy, to work with awarding bodies to ensure that the curricula delivered by the latter appropriately reflect the needs of the former. Changes in technology, working practices or consumer demand all have an impact on the world of work. In turn, any educational provision that purports to prepare individuals to enter that same world of work needs to be up to date, as do the tutors who deliver them (which partly explains the current emphasis on Continuing Professional Development (CPD) for tutors (discussed in Chapter 1)). Thus, SSCs, sometimes with other interested organizations such as professional or regulatory bodies, work alongside awarding bodies to ensure qualifications are both current and sufficient.

Current and recent curricular trends

An analysis of those trends that have shaped provision within the LLS over the medium or long term is beyond the scope of this present chapter. Debates about, for example, the relationship between vocational and academic curricula, and the social and political importance attached to each, go back over a hundred years. Once again, the reader is referred to the list of references that appear at the end of this chapter. However, there has been much recent activity (during the last four or five years or so) that has gone on to have a considerable impact on the curriculum as it is planned, delivered and experienced within the sector, and that have implications for practice in the near future. These are issues that do need to be discussed. But as we proceed, we have to be mindful of the more or less overt political narrative at work here (which we have already explored in Chapters 2, 3 and 4). Dealing with politically inspired change is nothing new. But the scale of policy-driven initiatives, targets, new qualifications and new professional partnerships that have shaped provision in the LLS within the past three or four years is quite considerable (Coffield et al., 2007). Here, then, we shall begin with a consideration of the impact of these changes on the curriculum, rather than a broader analysis of the policies and ideologies at work.

Task: staying up to date

Keeping up to date with policy initiatives and shifts can be a difficult task. The language of government policy is by no means clear or transparent, and it can be hard to find the time to read bulletins from the Learning and Skills Improvement Service (LSIS) or the *Times Educational Supplement* (*TES*) 'FE focus'. But staying informed about how government policy affects the curriculum within the LLS is important and worth while. Before reading on, take a look at the *TES* website, or the BBC Education News website, and think about how the issues raised in current news stories might have an impact on your professional practice.

Some of what has happened over the last few years can seem to be in some way removed from the curriculum as both tutors and students experience it. To take one example: for many tutors, notwithstanding the volume of CPD events and publicity materials, the lived reality of working under the *Every Child Matters* (*ECM*) framework (considering the Children Act of 2004 as our starting point) is simple. It generates another box or column to fill in on a college lesson plan when the Ofsted inspectors or other auditors come round. The debates and social policy issues that surround it are not necessarily forgotten or ignored: indeed, it could be argued that the *ECM* framework simply codified and organized a much more disparate set of policies and frameworks that were already in existence. And it would be unjust to argue that until *ECM*, tutors were *not* sensitive to the needs of their learners. But having new headlines such as 'enjoying and achieving' or 'making a positive contribution' does not *necessarily* lead to something novel or innovative. And so in the space of the experienced curriculum, as distinct from the planned curriculum, *ECM* is in a very real sense simply another policy to indicate acceptance of and acquiescence to, and this acceptance is made real in the audit trail, encapsulated perfectly by its inclusion within the Ofsted inspection framework for colleges (Ofsted, 2009: 36).

The 14–19 Agenda and the New Diplomas

Other recent changes in the direction of education policy can be seen as having a more tangible impact. The 14–19 Agenda encompasses changes to the curriculum as it is defined in the most generous sense, that is, as being concerned with every aspect of a course or programme of study: content, assessment, location, access and resources, including staff. In a way, the kinds of change being introduced are familiar: many tutors in the LLS are quite used to having to teach new things, to adapt materials, resources and strategies from one year to the next due to changes in the syllabuses that they are required to teach. Other innovations have been more novel: for example, the Education Maintenance Allowance (EMA). At one level, therefore, the 14–19 Diplomas simply represent yet another reason as to why a particular body of knowledge or skills has to be packaged and delivered differently in comparison to the last academic year. For some tutors in mainstream FE colleges, working with younger learners represents a more significant professional and personal challenge, and not solely because the QTLS curriculum is relatively quiet on the subject of 'working with 14–16s' (an expression invariably used by tutors and managers as a euphemism for managing classroom discipline). FE colleges have long been used to taking in the learners that nobody else wants or knows how to work with, and the 14–19 Agenda and the Diplomas are a natural extension of this, notwithstanding the impetus provided by the Leitch *Review of Skills* (2006), and despite stereotypical complaints about FE colleges being used by schools as dumping grounds for the learners that they do not want to teach, it would appear that for many young people, coming into FE does in fact represent a meaningful opportunity to learn and to work (Harkin, 2006). So what will Diplomas do differently in comparison to existing qualifications and progression routes? There are two ways to think about this: the practical and the pedagogical.

At a practical level, the mechanics of establishing new forms of working relationships between schools, colleges and employers would not seem insurmountable. And it surely makes sense to expand the provision of vocational or craft-based curricula for learners aged 14 or 15 who are disengaged, or at risk of disengaging, from mainstream education provision. Some of the logistical problems might not seem to have been thoroughly thought through: how these learners will travel to the different sites that deliver their learning is one important issue; how different schools and colleges will be able to synchronize their timetables is another. And as college tutors increasingly find themselves working with younger learners, issues of professional parity with schoolteachers, such as pay scales or teaching workloads, may begin to emerge. It is the extent of the Diplomas' success in encouraging more young people to stay in education or training for longer, and to experience greater levels of progression and success as they do so (which are key components of the government's 14–19 Agenda) that matter, and it will be some time before their success can be meaningfully evaluated. Nonetheless, the gradual (if rather partial) acceptance by universities of the Diploma as an entry qualification can be seen as vindicating, at some level, this aspect of the reforms enacted by the Labour government prior to 2010.

At a pedagogical level, the impact of the Diploma raises a number of interesting themes, although it is important to preface our discussion by remembering that to a significant degree, Diplomas have absorbed and reorganized, rather than rewritten, many existing qualifications. BTECs and 'A' levels, for example, now form part of the Diploma structure, but are otherwise unchanged. Diplomas are structured in three parts:

1   Principal learning (which relates to the specific occupational area that the Diploma rests in)
2   Generic learning (including functional skills)
3   Additional learning (optional components that allow an element of Diploma personalization).

We return to the topic of functional skills shortly. But there are other things to think about. Perhaps the most tangible pedagogical aspects of the Diploma are the different learning and teaching cultures that increasing numbers of 14–16 students might be expected to participate in. The environment of an FE college is quite different from that of a school, and practitioners in the FE sector hold teaching qualifications that rarely, if at all, pay specific heed to learning and teaching issues as they affect younger learners. In addition, each Diploma has to include a work experience period of at least 10 days in a 'real world environment'. How will what is learned during these placements be recognized and rewarded? Is it sufficient to assume that the provision of more flexible, work-related courses will help increase motivation and achievement among learners? Who is to say that a vocational or technical Diploma is 'the answer' to the problem of student disaffection and disengagement? What will the Diplomas actually do that current vocational or technical qualifications cannot do?

Functional skills

In the 10 years since the publication of the Moser Report, *A Fresh Start: Improving Literacy and Numeracy* (DfES, 1999), the development of literacy and numeracy skills has been a central, and much debated, component of provision within the learning and skills sector. Courses for younger learners at colleges for work-based learners and adults attending classes in community settings have benefited from new core curricula, new tranches of funding and newly qualified staff. And yet the nature of this provision continues to change and be changed: it would seem that barely a year goes by without a new literacy or numeracy initiative being launched by the appropriate government department or agency (which themselves change name and focus with sometimes bewildering speed). Thus, as teachers and trainers in the LLS, we find ourselves delivering functional skills, perhaps embedded within a GCSE or Diploma, or perhaps as a standalone qualification. But what are functional skills? The Qualifications and Curriculum Authority (QCA) defines them as follows: 'Functional skills are practical skills in English, Information and Communication Technology (ICT) and Mathematics, that allow individuals to work confidently, effectively and independently in life.'

The extent to which such a definition is satisfactory is open to question, however. Defining 'functional' is perhaps more complex than it might at first appear: 'Function must be defined in terms of that for which it is said to be functional, and that requires a detailed analysis of the job or mode of living for which the skills are needed' (Pring et al., 2009: 110).

So if functional skills are in some way contingent on the context within which they are to be employed or applied, then it might reasonably be argued that the functional skills required by, say, an electrician would be considerably different to those required by a hairdresser. To electrical installation and hairdressing tutors, this would probably not come as much of a surprise. Embedding functional skills within a specific technical or vocational curriculum would therefore seem to be a highly effective measure as it would provide a venue for the delivery of functional skills that are entirely relevant to, and meaningful to, the employment sector that the Diploma serves.

But this poses another problem for tutors. Who assesses functional skills? Do literacy and numeracy specialists, holding specific literacy or numeracy qualifications, have the kinds of expertise or understanding of the functional skills needs of different occupational sectors, or will a more generic approach to functional skills become apparent? Will the need to assess functional skills serve to distort the Diploma curriculum through, for example, the imposition of requirements for students to complete written work that is not constructively aligned to the industry or trade being followed?

Beyond further education: perspectives on lifelong learning

Finally, it is important to remember that an exploration of the curriculum within the LLS needs to take us beyond the confines of FE colleges, and into adult education centres, community centres, even factories and other places of work. When thinking about the wider sector, unfortunately, defining the curriculum within it becomes even more problematic. How are we to compare, for example, the provision of family history classes by the Workers' Educational Association (WEA) with the provision of English for speakers of other languages (ESOL) classes for migrant workers run by a charity such as the Five Lamps Organisation? Perhaps, appropriately, it is through changing definitions of lifelong learning, and through the disuse of other once common terms such as 'adult education' or 'continuing education', that changes in policy towards the provision of education and training for adults can be most straightforwardly discussed.

Changing priorities for the education of adults

The economic imperatives that are embodied within the Leitch (2006) *Review of Skills* also shape the ways in which lifelong learning is defined, funded and provided. It was not so long ago that local education authorities (LEAs), universities and charities offered a range of courses for adults that were seen as purely recreational (i.e. that did not carry a formal assessment burden or lead to a recognized qualification). The justification for such an approach, sometimes referred to as the *liberal tradition of adult education*, was that the process of encouraging participation in learning by adults who, for whatever reason, had not enjoyed success in compulsory schooling, was not to be jeopardized by an insistence on assessment and grading. Over the last 15 years or so, much of this kind of provision has vanished as government funding has been directed at the kinds of education and training provision for adults that are perceived as having economic, rather than personal or social, impact. This political shift was best summed up (though by no means initiated) in a speech delivered in 2006 by the then Secretary of State for Education and Skills, Alan Johnson MP:

> We must rebalance taxpayer's money towards the subjects where there is greatest need – so more plumbing, less pilates; subsidised precision engineering, not over-subsidised flower arranging, except of course where flower arranging is necessary for a vocational purpose. Tai chi may be hugely valuable to people studying it, but it's of little value to the economy. There must be a fairer apportionment between those who gain from education and those who pay for it – state, employer or individual.

> Surveys show that adults agree they should pay more for courses where they can. So colleges shouldn't have to cut courses just because budgets in some areas have been reduced. The trick is making sure courses appeal to students and employers – keeping demand, interest and quality high. With these principles at the heart of a re-energised further education system, it is entirely possible for colleges to increase fees and raise enrolments at the same time.

Early in 2009 John Denham, the then Secretary of State at the (now defunct) Department of Innovation, Universities and Skills (DIUS), caused considerable dismay when he referred to adult education classes as being nothing more than opportunities for people to learn Spanish before going on holiday. So, while learners under the age of 24 have benefited from new and innovative forms of provision and funding, adult learners have fared less well. According to the Campaigning Alliance for Lifelong Learning (CALL), two million adult learner places have been lost from the further and adult education sectors since 2005 as a consequence of course cutbacks and increased charges.

The learning revolution: time for a change?

With these political sentiments in mind, it is perhaps surprising to note the appearance, in March 2009, of a new government strategy for informal learning, laid out in a government *White Paper* called *The Learning Revolution*, which states:

> The boom in book clubs, on-line research and blogging, together with the continuing popularity of museums, public lectures and adult education classes, all demonstrate that people in this country have a passion for learning. They may not call it education, but this informal adult learning makes a huge contribution to the well-being of the nation. It is a revolution this Government is proud to foster and encourage.

> (DIUS, 2009: 4–5)

It might be churlish to point out that the continued survival of adult education classes is more in spite of, rather than because of, the policies of both the previous Labour and current Conservative/Liberal Democrat governments. It seems in keeping with the at times slavish devotion to e-learning displayed by government ministers that the paper refers to online research (perhaps family history?) and blogging. And, yes, these are all forms of learning. But do they have the same kinds of impact that more formalized adult education provision might have? Nonetheless, there is something to cheer in the *White Paper*. Among the initiatives planned to increase access to 'non-vocational learning where the primary purpose isn't to gain a qualification' can be found:

- plans to help non-commercial, voluntary 'self-starter' groups establish themselves and then access free or low-cost venues (such as museums or libraries)
- proposals to expand union learning and open 50 new union learning centres
- a £20 million 'transformation fund' to help establish new partnerships and forms of provision.

Successive governments have spent many years shifting the lifelong learning agenda so that it focuses more closely on the maintenance and enhancement of those employability skills that a flexible workforce has to have in order to remain competitive in a globalized economic system. This dominant perspective of lifelong learning is not concerned with continuing adult education as a vehicle for personal development, social cohesion or cultural stimulation. Rather, it is concerned with developing what Bernstein ([1996] 2000) referred to as 'trainability': the ability to cope with and profit from successive episodes of retraining and reskilling so as to be able to change occupational roles as and when needed.

It would be a mistake to think that the learning revolution is intended to take us back to the 'golden age' of liberal adult education. But it is nonetheless an important document, and one that could lead to a first, small change in attitude towards those forms of educational provision that do not directly lead to qualifications and enhanced workplace competencies, but that nevertheless do have important social and cultural benefits such as tackling social exclusion, maintaining mental health and engaging people across communities.

Implications for tutors working with adult learners

What might this all mean for tutors in adult education? It is hard to disagree with the philosophical tone of the learning revolution, but it is quite another for the different bureaucracies, organizations, quangos and funding bodies actually to implement such a permissive agenda. Nonetheless, there are some parts of the *White Paper* that hint at possible changes to working practices.

The curriculum and quality assurance – inspection

From September 2010, according to the *White Paper*, Ofsted will pilot a new regime for the inspection of informal learning, where the focus will be on assessing how well local partners are working together to provide innovative informal learning, widen participation and deliver 'positive outcomes'. For tutors working in adult education, the requirements of an Ofsted inspection represent a relatively recent change to working practices. It was only in 2007 that Ofsted took over the inspection of adult education, after the closure of the Adult Learning Inspectorate. Whatever its remit, the reality is that there will be a new inspection system for practitioners to both acclimatize and respond to.

The curriculum and provision – where learning happens

Perhaps one of the most interesting components of the *White Paper* is the stated aim to encourage partnerships between local organizations that can play a part in the provision of informal adult education, whether through the provision of space for classes to be run or resources that classes can use. Libraries, schools, FE colleges, museums and universities are all entreated to co-ordinate their activities on a regional basis.

The curriculum and course content – what gets 'taught'

From a personal point of view, the prospect of a sudden flowering of classes in local history, art, photography or conversational Italian is far from unpleasant. Not many years ago, FE colleges and community centres would have been populated by a variety of classes on most weekday evenings. Any initiative that helps to restore such provision is to be welcomed, whether staffed by professionals or well-organized volunteers. So we might anticipate an increase in what used to be called the 'liberal adult education curriculum', though not necessarily with a concurrent increase in demand for tutors in those subjects.

Conclusion

In this chapter we have considered a number of key points:

1   Concepts and models for exploring the curriculum
2   Ways in which the mainstream FE curriculum has been shaped in recent years, with a focus on 14–19 Diplomas and functional skills
3   The learning revolution, and possible implications for the adult education curriculum.

There are just a few of the political initiatives and factors that have affected contemporary curricular provision in the LLS, nor will they be the last. What is perhaps more important to bear in mind, rather than any specific knowledge of particular government schemes or initiatives, is the way in which policy can change the direction of provision within the LLS with sometimes remarkable speed: it is an area of educational provision that rests on shifting sands, and it is often only through the resilience of the tutors that the stability of the students' experience can be maintained.

References

Bernstein, B. ([1996] 2000) *Pedagogy Symbolic Control and Identity: Theory, Research, Critique*. Oxford: Rowman & Littlefield.

Coffield, F., Edward, S., Finlay, I., Hodgson, A., Spours, K., Steer, R. and Gregson, M. (2007) How policy impacts on practice and how practice does not impact on policy, *British Educational Research Journal*, 33(5): 723–41.

Department for Education and Skills (DfES) (1999) *A Fresh Start: Improving Literacy and Numeracy*. Available online at www.dfes.gov.uk

Department for Innovation, Universities and Skills (DIUS) (2009) *The Learning Revolution*. London: DIUS.

Harkin, J. (2006) Treated like adults: 14–16 year-olds in further education, *Research in Post-compulsory Education*, 11(3): 319–39.

HM Treasury (2006) *The Leitch Report: Prosperity for All in the Global Economy – World Class Skills*. London: HM Treasury.

Lifelong Learning UK (LLUK) (2006) *New Overarching Professional Standards for Teachers, Tutors and Trainers in the Lifelong Learning Sector*. London: LLUK.

Ofsted (2009) *Handbook for the Inspection of Further Education and Skills from September 2009*. London: Ofsted.

Pring, R., Hayward, G., Hodgson, A., Johnson, J., Keep, E., Oancea, A., Rees, G., Spours, K. and Wilde, S. (2009) *Education for All: The Future of Education and Training for 14–19 Year Olds*. London: Routledge.

Web-based resources

Campaigning Alliance for Lifelong Learning
www.callcampaign.org.uk/
Five Lamps Organisation
www.fivelamps.org.uk/index.php?q=home
The Learning revolution
www.dius.gov.uk/skills/engaging_learners/informal_adult_learning/white_paper
Workers' Educational Association (WEA)
www.wea.org.uk/

7   Research-led teaching in the lifelong learning sector

Chapter objectives

This chapter looks at the role that research can play in informing teaching and training practices within the lifelong learning sector (LLS). After considering the broader nature and role of educational research, this chapter goes on to consider the ways in which educational research can impact on classroom practice.

Professional standards

This chapter addresses the following professional practice standards for Qualified Teacher Learning and Skills (QTLS):

> **AS 4** **Reflection and evaluation of their own practice and their continuing professional development as teachers.**
>
> **AP 4.3** **Share good practice with others and engage in continuing professional development through reflection, evaluation and the appropriate use of research.**
>
> **BP 2.6** **Evaluate the efficiency and effectiveness of own teaching, including consideration of learner feedback and learning theories.**
>
> **CP 4.1** **Access sources for professional development in own specialist area.**

(LLUK, 2006)

Introduction

What images and ideas come to mind when you hear the word 'research'? When asking this question to past CertEd/PGCE and degree students, the answers that we have tended to receive were something like 'men in white coats' (always gender-specific, irrespective of the gender of the student), 'laboratories' and 'archives'. But we rarely received any responses or comments relating to the kinds of ways in which educational research is carried out. We always found this surprising, bearing in mind both the variety of ways in which school, college or university provision of different kinds is researched and the sheer quantity of educational research that is conducted. When moving on to discuss how and why changes have been made, and continue to be made, to how educational provision is organized, delivered and assessed, our students would frequently refer to the work done by universities – 'academics' – and how they influenced policy and practice, but once again there was relatively little awareness of the conduct of the research that underpins such academic work. And this is something of a shame. The amount of educational research that gets done is considerable, and its variety is astonishing. In addition, and most importantly, the ways in which such research becomes implemented as practice, or informs policy, is similarly noteworthy.

But it is not just the research done by university lecturers or research bodies such as the National Foundation for Educational Research (NFER) that needs to be considered: increasingly, classroom practitioners themselves are encouraged (notably through programmes of study such as CertEds/PGCEs or degrees and Continuing Professional Development (CPD)) to carry out their own investigations into classroom practice, using the same research paradigms. So, in a sense, research is something that anyone should be encouraged to do, and the findings of that research – however large or small in scale – are always of value when interpreted and acted on in an appropriate and meaningful fashion.

Theories, concepts, research and teaching

Familiarity with different theories or concepts, and the research that underpins them, is a common feature of teacher-training courses within the LLS. Theories of learning and teaching are a good place to start. Discussions about behaviourism and neo-behaviourism conjure up visions of Pavlov ringing a bell to make dogs salivate, Skinner putting rats in a cage or Piaget asking children to describe a collection of objects on a table. Images such as these neatly sum up the character of much early speculation about the nature of learning and instruction. The prevalence of psychology in education and teacher-training courses within the university curriculum today reminds us of these. Some of the ways in which we, as teachers and trainers, are encouraged to plan and develop our teaching continue to rest on psychological approaches to understanding learning, despite more recent, and in some ways highly persuasive, criticisms of such approaches. The continuing use of Bloom's taxonomy of learning as a way of formulating behavioural learning objectives is a good example of this.

The contrast between these kinds of research, and the kinds of research carried out by Jean Lave and Etienne Wenger (1991) before they wrote their book *Situated Learning*, or by Stephen Ball as he wrote *Beachside Comprehensive*, could not be more pronounced. These two works, as well as many others, rest on a very different kind of educational research. In these two examples, research was carried out using *ethnographic* methods: the kind of research that involves being among the people being studied, observing, walking and perhaps talking with them so as to make sense of particular aspects of their lives and activities, over the course of many months or even years. Rather than drawing on psychology, research such as this draws on a number of other academic disciplines: anthropology, sociology, politics and history. Such research has helped us to appreciate that so much that happens relating to what we understand to be 'learning' is not solely to do with what happens 'in the head'. Rather, there are many kinds of social, environmental and cultural factors that impact on learning, education and training.

It might be argued that the kinds of research carried out under the name of 'educational research' are so broad that describing them simply as 'educational' is somehow insufficient. By any account, educational research would appear to be a broad church. This is hardly surprising, bearing in mind the many different kinds of human activity that count as education, or learning, or teaching and the many different places in which they happen. A cursory search using IngentaConnect, or Google Scholar, would pull up research relating to informal, vocational, adult and early years education, and the list goes on. So what kinds of research are useful and meaningful to practitioners in the LLS? How can the sometimes obtuse findings of academic or professional researchers make themselves felt within teachers' professional lives?

Making sense of research

CertEd/PGCE students tend to encounter the *findings* of such research in two places: textbooks and journal articles. Sometimes, as is often the case with learning theories, the actual process of research is lost sight of, or only briefly mentioned. QTLS textbooks tend to spend more time discussing the consequences of, for example, an andragogical approach to facilitating learning than the actual research that Malcolm Knowles carried out in order to arrive at his hypothesis. Journal articles are perhaps an easier way to appreciate how research is actually carried out, and how the findings of that research might have implications for learning and teaching, as they frequently make explicit reference to the methods or methodologies that were used as the research was carried out. But they tend to be written by academics for other academics to read and critique, rather than for practitioners to read and then act on. Sometimes, the results of research do find their way into more readily accessible formats: publications such as the *Research and Practice in Adult Literacy (RAPAL)* journal. *Adults Learning*, published by the National Institute for Adult and Continuing Education (NIACE), frequently gives coverage to research findings that are written in what might be termed 'a more accessible genre', in comparison to academic journals (which often use jargon that can take time to get used to). More often, however, the application of research or theory is more or less hidden from view; that is, practitioners draw on theories (of one kind or another) in a tacit manner. For example, an adult education tutor may plan to deliver a course using a facilitator approach, seeking to draw on the experiences of the student group as a resource for learning. Such an approach can be described as a common feature of the repertoire of adult educators influenced by the liberal tradition. What adult educators may not realize is the extent of the theory and research (as seen in work by, for example, Jack Mezirow or Jerome Bruner) that underpins such an approach.

A further factor that from time to time counts against educational research is the scepticism with which it is sometimes treated. Research is sometimes described as doing nothing more than encouraging new fads or trends that provide little practical benefit in the workshop or classroom. This attitude is perhaps encouraged by the sheer quantity of educational research, and the proliferation of concepts, theories or models that are subsequently produced. It may also be encouraged as a consequence of the unrealistic ambitions of researchers and theorists who, by trying to create theories of learning or teaching that are all-encompassing, instead go on to oversimplify the complex interactions that take place in a classroom or college. In contrast to this, the idea that practitioners should be encouraged to carry out their own classroom-based research foregrounds the notion of 'what works' and rather than relying on grand theory, practitioners can carry out small-scale research and then formulate their own ideas.

Thus, just as what counts as educational research has changed and grown over time (a look through some recent journals will easily illustrate the diversity of subjects and approaches), so ideas about who might carry out work that can be termed 'research' has also changed. Rather than solely being the preserve of university-based academics or other professional researchers (e.g. the National Foundation of Educational Research (NFER)), educational research is increasingly being carried out by practitioners – teachers. There are several aspects to this shift. Partly, this is a response to broader debates about what counts as educational research, as already discussed: relatively small-scale investigations can claim to be good research if they are designed and conducted properly and need not involve expensive laboratories or many months spent doing observations and interviews. Partly, this is a response to the concern that research can be too remote from the real world of the classroom or workshop: research can be seen as lacking relevance or applicability. And partly, this shift encourages a more 'bottom-up' approach that empowers practitioners to generate their own knowledge and understanding, as opposed to merely acting on research done by professional researchers who can sometimes be seen as 'outsiders'.

It is also a response to changes in how the teacher-training curriculum is constructed. The professionalization of the teacher workforce in the LLS has in part been accomplished through the introduction of new standards and qualifications that require trainee teachers to study at university level, where familiarity with and use of theoretical knowledge is an established part of the curriculum. In addition, many courses now include elements of research in them which, in turn, reflects broader, current trends in education more generally: namely, that the knowledge student teachers can generate through their own research is as valid and as useful as the knowledge to be found in textbooks and journals.

From research to research-led teaching

So what does all this mean for practitioners in the LLS? There are three themes to consider here: (1) accessing and evaluating research literature; (2) using research to inform classroom practice; and (3) carrying out practitioner research. These are explored in turn.

Accessing and evaluating research literature

'Research literature' is a term that we use to refer to a variety of kinds, or genres, of publication. These might be books, journals, reports or government documents. These different publications tend to be written for a variety of audiences: for example, a scholarly monograph (an academic book that is about a single subject) would be intended to be read by both lecturers and perhaps some students as well. If the researchers wanted to ensure that their work reached a wider audience, they may produce other kinds of report such as briefing papers, professional publications or press releases to be used by journalists.

Case study: helping research to address a wide audience – the Literacies for Learning in Further Education project

The Literacies for Learning in Further Education project (LfLFE) was a research project that ran from 2004 to 2007, involving staff from two universities and four further education (FE) colleges. The aim of the project (in brief) was to explore the literacy practices of students in FE, and to explore how these might relate to, and perhaps even help with, the literacy practices that they would encounter during their studies. The LfLFE project rejects the transferable skills approach to literacy, arguing instead that there are many different kinds of literacy, and that these need to be understood in terms of their social context. A student that was perceived to be a reluctant writer, to have 'literacy problems' or a 'literacy deficit', might in fact be highly adept at using other kinds of literacy outside their college life: writing a diary, or texting friends and family, for example. The project organizers and researchers deliberately set out to ensure that their findings were available to different audiences. As such, a variety of publications have been produced over the last few years: lengthy articles in peer-reviewed academic journals; shorter articles in magazines aimed at professionals; books; web-based resources; and a DVD. Some of these resources are listed at the end of this chapter.

(Edwards and Smith, 2005; Edwards and Miller, 2008; Ivaniç et al., 2009)

It is a relatively simple task to access research-based materials. The LfLFE project, in keeping with other recent projects that are part of the Teaching and Learning Research Programme (TLRP) funded by the Economic and Social Research Council (ESRC), has published a number of useful resources online. These are freely accessible to all. Academic journals are usually available in the libraries of both colleges and universities, although university libraries usually have significantly larger collections. Organizations such as the Learning and Skills Improvement Service (LSIS) or the Learning and Skills Research Network (LSRN) both commission and publish relevant research: again, these research reports are usually freely available via the Internet. Media such as the *Times Educational Supplement* 'FE Focus' or the BBC Education website sometimes report on research. In fact, once you start to look for it, there is a tremendous amount of material available.

But there is only so much time in the day, and the working lives of college-based lecturers and adult education tutors are very busy. Tutors who are working towards a CertEd/PGCE will from time to time be asked to read journal articles, but for other staff there is not always the time available for reading academic journals, or even 'FE focus', on a regular basis. The new Institute for Learning (IfL) requirements for CPD may encourage greater participation, but 30 hours a year (for a full-time member of staff) is hardly sufficient to do justice to the wealth of material available. Even so, keeping up to date with research is highly desirable for two main reasons (although there are others): first, to inform classroom practice (and we return to this shortly); and second, to maintain interest, enthusiasm and engagement with the scholarship of teaching and learning which is, after all, a central component of our work.

Case study: suggestions for focused research

In recent years, our own students have often asked us questions along the lines of 'which things should I read if I don't have much time for studying'? This is a fair question, in fact: by far the majority of CertEd/PGCE students work either part or full time while studying on a part-time basis. Reconciling work and study commitments with family life make time for study all the more difficult to find. While it is in some ways undesirable to recommend some publications or sources over others, it is nonetheless the case that we do not have the time to read everything that we should. So in the understanding that this is a highly subjective and partial process, here is a short list of suggested places for reading research that we would at the present time recommend unreservedly to tutors in the LLS. These choices are based on feedback from students as well as a consideration of the kinds of subject area that are covered by these different publications.

Academic journals:

- *Journal of Further and Higher Education*
- *Journal of Vocational Education and Training*
- *Research in Post-Compulsory Education*
- *Studies in the Education of Adults*

Other publications:

- *RAPAL Bulletin*
- *Adults Learning*

Website

- BBC Education website

Using research to inform classroom practice

Using research to inform classroom practice is not new. It might seem an obvious thing to say, but we shall say it nonetheless: what we understand teaching, training or learning to be does not stand still. The simplest way to witness the impact of educational research on classroom practices is to look inside some classrooms, and compare them to images of classrooms from 50 or even 100 years ago. To some extent, changes in educational practices have been driven by broader social, cultural and even technological factors: new curricular subjects (as discussed in Chapter 6) sometimes demand new forms of provision, new resources or new methods of teaching. Other changes in the work done by teachers and trainers can more directly be seen as a consequence of educational research. One relatively recent example is *assessment for learning*, based on research done into formative assessment practices by Paul Black and Dylan Wiliam that was first published a little over 10 years ago. Arguably, the discussion about the role of formative assessment and feedback that Black and Wiliam helped to kindle has influenced assessment practices across educational sectors. In turn, their initial research has led to a flowering of other research projects, journal articles and textbooks. The LfLFE project that we referred to above is another example of how educational research might impact on practice. Currently, however, there has yet to be any meaningful evaluation of any significant impact made by the LfLFE project on teaching practices within colleges.

Waiting for new educational tides to wash over us is one way of changing educational practices, but it is not the only one. And it is somewhat passive, conjuring up ideas of a teaching workforce that simply waits to be told by someone what the 'current thinking' is about a particular learning issue and how teachers should use it in the workshop or classroom. Here, we advocate a more active, agentive approach. By this, we mean that teachers and trainers need to be encouraged to access research literature more regularly, to experiment with what they do in the workshop or classroom, and to be willing to try new approaches to resources or assessments, or even how they talk and write with their students. In some senses, this can be seen as a creative approach to learning and teaching, although the broader 'creativity in education' agenda is not one that we uncritically subscribe to (and has been effectively critiqued by, among others, Simmons and Thompson (2008)). But we would also argue that the active use of such research encapsulates important components of professionalism: professional development (above and beyond mechanistic notions of compulsory CPD), and the use of theoretical, specialist knowledge to do our work (Tummons, 2007).

Using research to explore learners' behaviour outside class

'What are we doing when we read? Adult Literacy Learners' Perceptions of Reading' was published in *Research in Post-Compulsory Education* (Duncan, 2009). It provides an account of research carried out among adult literacy students in London. It is an example of *practitioner research*; that is, it is a piece of research that has been carried out by a classroom practitioner (the author, Sam Duncan, is an adult literacy teacher) with the development and possible improvement of classroom practice as an overt goal of the project. It is the kind of article that we encourage our own students to read: as well as reporting on the research itself, it also includes useful information about how the research was conducted and how the data was gathered and analysed (method and methodology). The article concludes by presenting a number of points that could inform teaching and learning in adult literacy contexts.

Just one of the points raised by Duncan provides us with a number of ways in which we can consider how research can inform classroom practice (and a careful reading of the entire piece is strongly recommended). Among the issues she raises at the end of the article is: 'Reading requires time. Some learners may not have enough time to read at home and therefore may need more class time allocated to reading' (Duncan, 2009: 329).

This statement raises a number of further questions: what does this mean for how we plan our lessons? What can we expect our learners to do between classes? Is this an issue that affects other curriculum areas as well as adult literacy?

The amount of time and space that learners have available to them at home to supplement the work that they do within formal educational settings has been the subject of other educational research. One of the most well-known writers on this subject is Basil Bernstein, and although his research focused on schools rather than colleges, it is still relevant to our current discussion. In his book *The Structuring of Pedagogic Discourse*, Bernstein wrote:

> Curricula cannot be acquired wholly by time spent at school. This is because the pacing of the acquisition [this is the rate at which learning is expected to occur] is such that time at school must be supplemented by official pedagogic time at home [...] As the pupil gets older he/she is expected to do more and more school work in the home, and the family will be expected to ensure that the pupil has time at home for this work [...] The basis of homework is usually a textbook. But the textbook requires a context, an official pedagogic context in the home. That is, a space – a silent space – and this is not usually available in the homes of the poor.
>
> (Bernstein, 1990: 77)

It is important to note that Duncan, and Bernstein before her, are not the only authors to make links between social and economic factors, and educational achievement. What these examples serve to remind us of is the fact that such factors affect learners at many different stages of life: both children, in compulsory schooling, and adults who have chosen (for all sorts of reasons) to return to learning. Thus, having considered the issue of the organization of learners' home lives, in terms of the time and space that might be available for study, how might practitioners then approach planning and preparation for their own learners?

Time and space for homework, and some practical considerations for tutors

If a group of students only meets for one morning or evening each week, the desirability of encouraging private study in between class time is obvious. Common sense (often under-represented in books about learning and teaching) as well as theory would seem to suggest that doing some work in between sessions will help reinforce the learning that takes place in class, notwithstanding any more formal requirements for private study that the curriculum might be seeking to impose. And the demands for students to be able to plan their own private study outside class time are arguably being further increased by the provision of e-learning routes within many programmes of study. A quiet time and place for private study are undeniably important, but they are not always easily available. So, how might tutors in the LLS be able to facilitate private study, or plan for those learners for whom attending class is the only opportunity for study that they have access to?

The following points are not intended to be exhaustive or definitive, rather, they are intended as points for discussion and perhaps reflection.

- Study skills books that talk about time management are all well and good, but they rarely reflect the complexities of some learners' lives. Some learners do have space at home, or at work, for regular study, but some do not. Despite all our exhortations, some students will work on a 'famine or feast' basis, and will have fluctuating amounts of time available for reading and preparing. As such, as tutors we need to be prepared for the fact that students may be well-prepared for one session, and ill-prepared the next.
- Spending time thinking about creative responses to students' needs is always worth while. Engendering peer support groups among students can be beneficial. Finding out about other places where students can go to study is another. If the curriculum will allow it, programming a reading week can be helpful (although we have to be realistic and assume that not all students will use it in the way it is intended).
- The unpredictability of daily life will invariably take precedence over study goals and assignment deadlines. Whether we work with adult learners, or 14–16 learners, as tutors we need to be sensitive to such pressures and mindful of their impact on students' classroom behaviour and our classroom practices.

Carrying out practitioner research

Reading accounts of other peoples' research in books or journals is both interesting in itself and helpful to our professional practice. But our engagement with research need not stop there. Actually doing some educational research, even on a small scale, can be both personally and professionally rewarding and may even lead to more extensive research activity. Many tutors in the LLS now find themselves doing small-scale research as part of a formal programme of study or for CPD purposes. Indeed, in 2009, the IfL established the *Hewett/Driver Action Research Bursaries*, worth £1,000, targeted specifically for 'individual practitioner research', and which is available to anyone who works in FE or work-based learning (WBL) contexts. In addition, the IfL website includes 'a brief introduction to action research', providing a short but nonetheless quite useful theoretical background to the ways in which practitioners might undertake their research projects.

A brief note on terminology may be useful here, as we have now used three different terms to describe this kind of research: small-scale research; practitioner research; and action research. There are other variants as well including critical action research, participatory action research and classroom research. While there are some (more or less fine) distinctions to be drawn between these different kinds of research, they all share a few key characteristics. Here, we use the term 'practitioner research', by which we mean:

- research that is carried out by classroom practitioners (as distinct from professional researchers) and is about their own teaching
- research that is focused on everyday teaching and learning practices and that seeks to develop, improve or otherwise shed new light on some aspect of these practices
- research that is driven by the practitioner; that is, the choice of research topic is made by the teacher or trainer
- research that is local in scope, that is, the research carried out does not claim to be universally applicable, but is deliberately focused on the context within which the practitioner works
- research that is carried out using appropriate and relevant methods and methodologies.

Typically, such small-scale projects might concern themselves with the implementation of new assessment strategies, or new forms of classroom design, or new teaching resources (although these are by no means the only possible topics for such research). The project would therefore involve an analysis of the new strategy in question, a consideration of the rationale that lies behind it (which in turn would rest on an appreciation of wider research literature on the same or a similar subject), and an evaluation of its impact on the students.

It is important to note that although such research is usually carried out on a local and small-scale basis, the demands placed on it in terms of method and methodology are as important as they would be for a large-scale research project that might take place over a much longer period of time (such as a PhD, for example). That is to say, any such research would need to be carefully and rigorously planned and carried out, and care would need to be taken over how the results might be interpreted and how they might impact on practice. Relevant ethical issues would also have to be addressed. Some examples of projects carried out by students that we have worked with in recent years include:

- the role information communication technology (ICT) plays in educational settings, enabling pupils to engage in literacy development and thereby boosting self-esteem
- assessment for learning, and how it is valued by teachers and learners in geography classes
- the behaviour exhibited by learners in post-compulsory settings
- fire marshal and fire safety training: an investigation into the delivery of fire safety training in a work-based setting
- the experiential learning of 14–19-year-old students in a realistic work environment.

It is the last example of these that we focus on to provide a worked example of how a practitioner researcher used appropriate research methods and methodologies.

Case study: the experiential learning of 14–19-year-old students in a realistic work environment

Peter is a lecturer in catering and hospitality at a large urban further education (FE) college. After completing his Cert Ed, he decided to study for a top-up degree. During his CertEd, he became interested in theories of experiential learning (such as David Kolb's experiential learning cycle) and theories of learning as socially situated within communities of practice (drawing on the work of Etienne Wenger). As such, when it came to choosing a topic for his practitioner research project for his degree, he already knew what he wanted to do.

Peter is interested in the impact of environment on learning. Having moved into new college buildings (as part of the new build programme funded by the Learning and Skills Council (LSC)), his students now had access to a range of new facilities, including new training kitchens and a new training restaurant. Satisfied that these facilities would enhance the learning of practical skills, he wanted to know whether or not working in these new realistic work environments would also enhance theoretical learning as well. And so he designed a curriculum that saw some of the students covering the theory-based course content in the kitchens, and others covering them in standard college classrooms. After several weeks, he swapped the groups over, then after a few more weeks, he talked with the learners about their experiences of studying the theoretical components of the course in two different physical environments. He used two methods to gather data: observation (keeping a notebook throughout); and focus groups to gather student feedback (having considered individual interviews, but ruled them out as being too time-consuming), which were recorded and then transcribed.

In his notebook, Peter made frequent notes referring to how the students behaved. There seemed to be significantly better behaviour among students when they were in the training kitchens than when they were in the classroom. Behaviour was better, timekeeping was better and there was a real sense of greater engagement: the sessions felt more lively and there was much more animated conversation about the subjects being studied. In the focus groups, the students echoed these observations, stating a preference for learning theoretical content in the training kitchens because being in the kitchens helped them to make sense of what they were being asked to remember. By covering the underpinning knowledge in a practical setting, students could make links between factual information and the tasks that accompanied it.

The limits of practitioner research

Peter's project confirmed what he had already supposed: that the environment offered in the practical setting of a training kitchen was more conducive to learning than a classroom with tables and chairs. As such, his findings reinforced much other educational research (in many cases, of considerably larger scale) relating to environment and its impact on learning. Indeed, the extent to which new research 'fits in' or complements existing research is often seen as a key criterion of research quality (Flick, 2008). At the same time, we need to be aware of the limitations of the action research approach. Among common criticisms of action research can be found:

- Subjectivity: data collection, analysis and interpretation are all carried out by an individual (or group of individuals, in a collaborative project) who are exploring their own actions and motives. How critical or honest can the researcher be in such situations? Can they always see the wood for the trees?
- Formality: larger-scale research projects invariably have to go through a rigorous approval process, which is not necessarily present in small-scale research. The fact that such action research projects are responsive to local conditions and needs is taken to imply a lack of rigour, compared to the extensive planning and preparation that a formal 'academic' or 'professional' researcher would carry out.

Is there any justification in these criticisms? To an extent, the answer must be 'yes'. But these criticisms can also be levelled at more extensive or detailed research projects.

Case study: participatory action research

In our own participatory action research, we have shared and disseminated our findings on a local, national and international level. And, most importantly, we have provided a platform for our adult learners to share their stories. A driving factor behind this was to facilitate learners in taking ownership of the whole research process, from beginning to conclusion. Part of this process included the learners themselves, rather than the researchers, addressing an international conference, relating their accounts of what makes a good teacher:

> I will say to become better teachers, be an inspiration, a good educational role model. Have empathy, patience, humility, and a genuine concern for students, and please never give up on them: their greatest work is yet to come. Sometimes a teacher may not just develop reading or writing skills. You are developing a person who might never have been in an educational or classroom environment for a very long time and it could be new for them.
>
> (Johnson et al., 2010)

The acquisition of literacy skills – the subject of the research – is strongly bonded to the creation of knowledge and by employing an action research approach, the learners and the researchers were able to reveal stories of marginalized groups that had historically been silenced. In doing so the literacy classes and the research offered a critical space for the learners to become more active in their own learning, regardless of their previous histories or experiences (Duckworth, 2010).

Many academics, writing on the subject of research method and methodology, have questioned not only the existence but also the desirability of objectivity in research. Others have pointed out that being prepared to adapt or change research plans in the light of changing conditions in the research field, sometimes referred to as 'researcher reflexivity', need not be a problem as long as any changes are properly recorded and discussed. In short, it can be said that there are no foolproof or perfect ways to do educational research. Action research is just one of several approaches that should be adhered to if it is the right approach to take by practitioners who are mindful of both its strengths and its limitations.

There are many books about the conduct and interpretation of practitioner or action research (and, indeed, about educational research more generally), and some suggestions for further reading appear at the end of this chapter.

Conclusion

Reading, and reflecting on, research in education – whether published recently or not – can help our classroom practice, stimulate our imaginations and enhance our professionalism. And it can take you in unexpected directions. The research journeys of both of the authors of this book began several years ago when both Vicky and Jonathan worked in FE colleges. Both Vicky's research (in adult literacy) and Jonathan's research (in assessment practices) were inspired by their experiences as classroom practitioners. In one sense, research can even be emancipatory, allowing you to travel in directions that might not initially seem possible. And although it can be difficult to find the time, resources or energy to carry out research, it must surely be in the interests of all tutors in the LLS to be aware of the research that is being done so that our teaching can stay fresh, challenging and rewarding.

References

Bernstein, B. (1990) *Class, Codes and Control Volume IV: The Structuring of Pedagogic Discourse*. London: Routledge.

Duckworth, V. (2010) Sustaining Learning Over Time: It Looks More Like a Yellowbrick Road Than a Straightforward Path for Women Experiencing Violence. *Research and Practice in Adult Literacy*, 71: 26–7.

Duncan, S. (2009) 'What are we doing when we read?' Adult literacy learners' perceptions of reading, *Research in Post-Compulsory Education*, 14(3): 317–31.

Edwards, R. and Miller, K. (2008) Academic drift in vocational qualifications? Explorations through the lens of literacy, *Journal of Vocational Education and Training*, 60(2): 123–31.

Edwards, R. and Smith, J. (2005) Swamping and spoonfeeding: literacies for learning in further education, *Journal of Vocational Education and Training*, 57(1): 47–60.

Flick, U. (2007) *Managing Quality in Qualitative Research*. London: Sage Publications.

Ivanič, R., Edwards, R., Barton, D., Martin-Jones, M., Fowler, Z., Hughes, B., Mannion, G., Miller, K., Satchwell, C. and Smith, J. (2009) *Improving Learning in College: Rethinking Literacies Across the Curriculum*. London: Routledge.

Lave, J. and Wenger, E. (1991) *Situated Learning: Legitimate Peripheral Participation*. Cambridge: Cambridge University Press.

Johnson, C., Duckworth, V., McNamara, M. and Apelbaum, C. (forthcoming) A tale of two adult learners: from adult basic education to degree completion, *NADE Digest*.

Lifelong Learning UK (LLUK) (2006) *New Overarching Professional Standards for Teachers, Tutors and Trainers in the Lifelong Learning Sector*. London: LLUK.

Simmons, R. and Thompson, R. (2008) Creativity and performativity: the case of further education, *British Educational Research Journal*, 34(5): 601–18.

Tummons, J. (2007) *Becoming a Professional Tutor in the Lifelong Learning Sector*. Exeter: Learning Matters.

8 Working in the lifelong learning sector

Chapter objectives

This chapter looks at the new professional framework for teachers: Qualified Teaching and Learning Status (QTLS) and the Institute for Learning (IfL). It explores the role/expectations of a professional in the lifelong learning sector (LLS) and what impact this may have on your responsibilities and legislative requirements. It also examines balancing home and work life in order to get the most out of your teaching and personal time. To support this it considers effective time management skills and working effectively in a team.

This chapter addresses the following professional practice standards for QTLS:

AK 5.1 **Ways to communicate and collaborate with colleagues and/ or others to enhance learners' experience.**

AK 6.1 **Relevant statutory requirements and codes of practice.**

AP 7.1 **Keep accurate records which contribute to organisational procedures.**

BK1.3 **Ways of creating a motivational learning environment.**

BK 2.6 **Ways to evaluate own practice in terms of efficiency and effectiveness.**

BP 4.1 **Collaborate with colleagues to encourage learner progress.**

FK 3.1 **Progression and career opportunities within own specialist area.**

(LLUK, 2006)

Introduction: the new professional framework for QTLS and the IfL

The teaching qualifications for further education (FE) staff have been broadened to embrace all those teaching in the LLS. This reform was initially brought to the fore in the Department for Education and Skills (DfES, 2004) document *Equipping our Teachers for the Future* in which it identified two agencies as being essential players in the reforms framework. They are LLUK and the Institute for Learning (IfL). LLUK is the sector skills council responsible for the professional development of all of us working in the field of lifelong learning. It supports learning providers in meeting the challenges of the current skills and education agendas and has replaced the Further Education National Training Organisation (FENTO).

The reforms apply to all the Learning and Skills Council (LSC) funded areas including FE, work-based learning, voluntary and community organizations and also museums, libraries and archives. It aims to raise the status of practitioners across the sector by, among other things, meeting recognized standards of practice. The reforms require all new tutors to achieve an introductory teaching qualification in order to practice, known as Preparing to Teach in the Lifelong Learning Sector (PTTLS) and achieve a full teaching qualification that includes the Certificate in Teaching in the Lifelong Learning Sector (CTTLS) and the Diploma in Teaching in the Lifelong Learning Sector (DTLLS) within five years. The DfES named the IfL as the body that awards the 'licence to practice' as QTLS. All new teachers will need to join the IfL in order to obtain QTLS status and a licence to practice. They will also need to record their continuing professional development (CPD) with IfL if they wish to remain licensed practitioners. Existing teachers will also be required to have their CPD recorded and are also required to join IfL and maintain a licence to practice. The Code applies to all members of the Institute and the aim of the enforcement is to protect the interests of learners and the wider public. It is subject to regular reviews to ensure that it remains relevant and reflects progress in professional practice (see www.ifl.ac.uk/professional-standards/code-of-professional-practice).

The thrust is that FE teachers will benefit from a strong, autonomous, highly respected and nationally recognized professional body that can lead to high expectations and standards of conduct and competency, regulate the FE teaching profession, improve professional development opportunities in line with the 30 hours CPD (pro rata), which are required to maintain a licence to practice, give direction on teaching and learning issues and provide a stage for practitioners' voices. Interestingly, the IFL's 'code of professional practice' does not refer to the LLUK overarching professional standards. Contentious by its absence, this may suggest that competency-based teacher-training approaches are redundant on qualifying, replaced instead by models of CPD where autonomy is at the apex of practice. In addition, FE lecturers employed to teach basic, essential or functional skills are required to hold or work towards a specialist Skills for Life teaching qualification in literacy, numeracy or English for speakers of other languages (ESOL).

The Institute for Learning states that: 'The Institute for Learning values and promotes the autonomy of learning practitioners whilst aiding their individual and collective development within a framework of integrity, honesty and professionalism' (IfL Handbook).

These relate to six core principles:

- integrity
- respect
- care
- practice
- disclosure
- responsibility.

Bridging the divide between subject specialism and pedagogy

In the move towards achieving the standards in qualifying to teach, there is an expectation for practitioners to develop a unity of subject specialist knowledge and pedagogy for the effective promotion, delivery and evaluation of best practice. The acquiring and developing of your pedagogy may also help you to have an understanding of your learners and their experience of acquiring new subject-specific knowledge. This awareness can facilitate the recognition of the barriers learners may face when commencing a new discipline.

For example, getting to grips with a new subject-specific meta-language can prove a real barrier and challenge for many learners. This is not dissimilar from the feelings many trainee teachers encounter when they are initially faced with the meta-language of education.

In the following case study, Roy, a specialist in business, shares his experience.

Case study

With a Degree and Masters in business I felt fully competent to fly through the teacher education course. I had successfully developed a thorough knowledge of my specialism in business. Indeed, when I was working for a highly charged business company in order to communicate effectively with colleagues and clients it was essential that I was confident in my specialist language skills. What I wasn't prepared for was the need to learn the language of education. After the first couple of lectures I knew I would need to be confident in the use of the new words/terminologies being taught in the class in order to communicate effectively about my practice. At first I was baffled by such words as androgogy or putting meaning to procedures such as assessment records, screening and diagnostic reports etc. Experiencing this barrier to language made me fully realise the barriers my learners face when they begin a business course. Now I think of the strategies which helped me to develop my language acquisition skills in pedagogy and apply them in my own lessons to help my learners grasp the new terminology being taught; it's about putting myself in their shoes.

What are your role and expectations?

FE encompasses full- or part-time, academic or vocational learning or training for those traditionally over the age of 16 in a number of college and community settings. However, with the drive for a collaborative approach between colleges and schools and the New Diploma at its centre, there is now a move towards 14–16-year-olds being taught in FE colleges by FE staff. In light of the disparity between a school teacher's and an FE teacher's wage, this is a contentious issue for many – the question being, why is the FE teacher paid less but expected to take on the same role and responsibility as a school teacher? If wage reflects value, which is the case in an economic-driven culture, how does this position the FE teacher? In addition, teachers with PGCE (FE) qualifications may still only be employed by schools as 'instructors', whereas teachers with Qualified Teacher Status (QTS) for teaching students of school age may teach in any school or college setting. Legislation is clearly needed to tackle how best teachers with the PGCE (FE) qualification may be given QTS and how QTLS leads to parity of wage and conditions. This has implications for courses of Initial Teacher Education and Training that lead to a PGCE (FE) qualification being adjusted to take account of the new 14–16 contexts in which lecturers are required to teach in schools and colleges.

Meeting the targets

As trainee teachers and qualified practitioners target setting is an integral part of your teacher-training programme and future practice. Targets can be identified from a number of sources and situations. A key driver for target setting relates to developing, implementing and evaluating improvements to your practice. These targets may be set by members of your department including your mentor, subject coach, programme manager or yourself. The targets set can also relate to the measurement of the retention and achievement of your learners against national benchmarks. The pressure to meet benchmarks, get learners through exams, and source funding can cause a dilemma for practitioners. It erodes a tutor's autonomy to develop a curricula and qualifications where all learning achievements are valued equally (Hyland and Merrill, 2003) and instead creates real pressure to achieve 'hard' targets defined by 'qualifications'. Following this model, teaching and learning often does not measure anything outside a competency-based approach, where the curriculum is imposed on a learner from above rather than being driven by them and their own needs and aspirations. With such external pressures, professional integrity can be undermined. Indeed, as busy professionals it is often easier to churn out prescriptive lessons without striving for new critical approaches that support personalized approaches to teaching and learning, and challenge both the individual practitioner and the student group.

Location

When considering the location and settings in the LLS, it is important to be aware that these are diverse and may include:

- places of worship: churches, synagogues, temples, mosques and so on
- prisons
- specialist adult education centres
- community and voluntary projects
- unions
- workplace settings
- schools
- local community centres
- Sure Start Centres
- refuges for the homeless
- hostels
- further education colleges and universities.

Types of course

The types of course being developed and delivered within these contexts will vary to meet the needs of the cohort. Courses can offer a first step to further study; for example, Skills for Life provision, which may lead to work or training, vocational courses or access into higher education (HE) programmes and university. Learners can in fact go on truly inspirational learning journeys.

Case study: from adult literacy class to higher education

One of Vicky's former literacy learners, Marie, struggled to read and write when she began her literacy course at an FE college in the north-west of England. A single mum with three children, Marie's six-year learning trajectory is shown in Fig. 8.1:

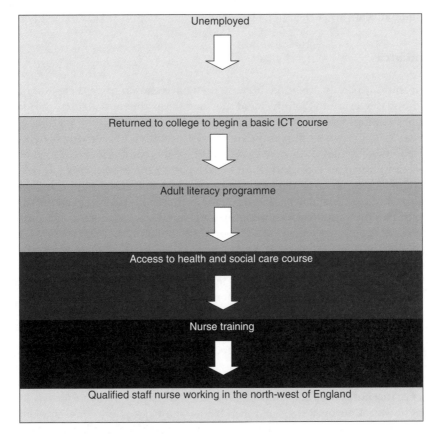

Figure 8.1   Marie's learning trajectory

Knowing your learners

Clearly, adult learners do not arrive through the college doors as blank templates they arrive with a history of learning that may be located within traditional educational routes, for example, GCSEs and 'A' levels, or gained in their everyday social practices, for example, balancing their household accounts, caring for a family, decorating the home and so on. Some may step onto a course after leaving school early with few or no qualifications while others may return to the classroom with degrees. As such they will have had very different life experiences and educational trajectories. Many adults attend adult literacy, numeracy or ESOL classes for personal development as well as a stepping stone onto other pathways. Some learners may want to learn another language or develop skills within the creative field such as a life drawing class or flower arranging. They may be teenagers or mature learners, employed or unemployed, parents, carers or homeless, drug addicts or alcohol-dependent.

The vital thing is to recognize and acknowledge that groups of learners are not homogenous in terms of background, age, knowledge and motivation but bring with them a diversity of skills and experience that they have acquired in their private and public domains of their life.

Attendance

Adult learners generally attend FE because they have chosen to be there and because the learning is relevant to their lives and they have clear aims and objectives. However, there are situations where adults attend courses that are compulsory: training courses in the workplace or where they must attend as a condition of receiving benefits such as education maintenance allowance (EMC). Where it is compulsory to attend lessons, learners can sometimes lack motivation to take part in the lesson. This can be a challenge for the learner and the teacher. A lack of interest and engagement can stem from a number of causes: one may be that the learners' have experienced negative labelling at school. This can result in low self-esteem and confidence. In order to address this or other reasons for disengagement, it is important to build on the learners' aims, aspirations, motivations and interests. This can help to create a critical space where they can explore and make sense of events that may have held them back.

In the following case study, Kath Taylor, a grandmother and former literacy learner, was triggered to write poetry on her course.

Case study: literacy learning through writing poetry

When I started a part-time course, I never in my wildest dreams thought I'd write poems. I felt out of my league. My tutor reassured me, saying words are for everyone then slowly taking small steps and then bigger and bigger I grew braver. Words I never thought I'd use sprang out of my head and onto the page. When I am feeling stressed about something I find it good therapy to put my thoughts and feelings on paper in the form of a poem. I wish I would have had this outlet when I was younger and life hit hard. But what matters is I've proved life gets better with age if you have the tool to help you find your way – for me the tools are the words in my poetry.

(Duckworth and Taylor, 2008: 30–2)

Task

Identify the teaching and learning strategies you may need to put in place to meet the diverse needs of learners in the LLS. If there are strategies you want to develop further you may want to consider: *why – how – when – where –* and *who* can help you do this.

Securing work

Jobs in the LLS are available in a variety of establishments, not only in FE colleges or sixth forms, but locations such as in the prison service, the armed forces education unit and company training departments. There are some opportunities in training organizations that offer vocational and Skills for Learning training to young people and adults as well as private training companies that also offer work-based skills training.

Competition for posts varies according to the subject offered and the part of the country where work is sought. Many contracts are for temporary and part-time work but both are good ways of getting a first job and developing contacts. Most part-time positions are advertised in the local newspapers and some colleges place an advert for part-time staff usually in March and the following few months for the start of the academic year. Jobs can also be obtained by sending a CV to the head of department on a speculative basis: let them see you are keen and a go-getter. Placements, visits, shadowing and voluntary work are useful for networking and for gaining access to jobs that are not advertised. Many FE lecturers work for a number of organizations, sometimes on short-term contracts, while also pursuing their specialist area in other ways outside education. They may, for example, teach hairdressing and work in a salon or work as an accountant and teach accountancy.

Work for teachers of FE can often be secured through an agency and be on a part-time basis. This may suit people who have other commitments: for example, retired tutors who want to keep 'their hand in' or others who may have child care responsibilities. There is full-time work available, but increasingly this is seen as the next step after agency work.

Securing a permanent position

Building up your knowledge and skills is a key to securing a permanent position. Once in a new role it will certainly bring responsibilities outside teaching. This may mean working collaboratively within your department, across faculties and in multidisciplinary areas. An example may include becoming involved in cross-college projects such as sharing best practice on how to embed diversity across the specialist areas. In order to secure employment in the LLS you may want to consider the skills you have and how they can develop over your career.

Task: career planning

Identify your growing responsibilities as a trainee teacher or a qualified member of the team. Arrange a meeting with your mentor/curriculum manager or another member of the teaching team and ask them to outline their responsibilities. Compare their role to yours. This will offer you an indication of how your role will develop as your career lengthens.

Compliance with legislative requirements

As with any area of work, tutors must work within the boundaries of the law and professional values. Your organization will have its own policies and procedures relating to these legal requirements. As a trainee or qualified member of the teaching team, your induction will offer you the opportunity to meet the staff you will be working alongside and familiarize yourself with the settings policy and procedures. For those of you who are in-service you may have an induction in another area in order to broaden your teaching timetable and skills and knowledge. In order to work effectively in the LLS you need to have a keen awareness of the current legislation and codes of practice that are deemed relevant to your subject specialism and the organization you are on placement/employed. There are a large number of laws and professional ethics that are constantly being updated. You should ensure you know where these are stored and familiarize yourself with them.

Task: exploring policy

Identify two policies where you are on placement/employed. What impact do these have on teaching and learning in your specialist area?

Record keeping

You will no doubt encounter a mountain of paperwork and tackling it promptly and effectively will be required in your role as a professional in the LLS. As such, ensuring up to date and accurate record keeping are essential parts of your day-to-day practice. Learners' records need to be kept safe; there are requirements that fall under the Data Protection Act to protect the confidentiality of both learners and staff. Failure to adhere to the policy and procedures of your work can be classed as gross misconduct in many organizations. The majority of legislation and codes of practice offer a firm framework within which practitioners can effectively work in a safe and fair environment.

Working within a multidisciplinary team

To meet the needs of your learners, you will almost certainly be required to work effectively in a team. This team may include members of staff in your subject-specific area and department together with people across the wider multidisciplinary areas. Having colleagues to share ideas, best practice and struggles with can help to create a real supportive and motivating environment leading to a satisfying and rewarding work life.

Quality of teaching

The subject area in which you are on placement or are employed can be a strong factor in determining the quality of teaching and learning in the area you are based. Working in a professional community can offer you the opportunity to share best practice.

The following case study focuses on Sharon who is a trainee teacher, and a specialist in health studies.

Case study: good practice in health studies in further education

As a trainee teacher I would spend most weekends developing resources for my groups. Working alone, I found it isolating and sometimes found it difficult to decide what approaches to use. For example when I planned to deliver a session on 'healthy eating' I had lots of ideas on how to teach the topic to a class of 16 year olds. I toyed with the idea of the learners creating menus and perhaps bringing in food magazines. Then I thought about showing them different types of fresh foods – perhaps having them taste the more exotic. I only had one hour to deliver the session and with so many choices I found it difficult to decide what to use and which approach to take. When I began to discuss my dilemma in the staff room a number of the tutors said they felt the same about planning their lessons. We began to share our ideas and experiences over our lunch breaks. From the pool of ideas the discussions raised I was able to feed the valuable input from other practitioners into my lessons. I opted for asking the learners to create healthy eating posters and displaying them on the classroom walls. I couldn't resist also bringing in exotic fruit and vegetables for the group to taste – for many this had been the first time they had tried such fruits as lyches and sweet potatoes. The feedback from the class was very positive – learning clearly took place. I shared the impact with my fellow practitioners. We all now regularly share strategies and approaches. I feel it helps us all to develop our skills, practice and confidence in a meaningful way.

Professional communities

As a practitioner in the LLS, critical reflection plays a crucial part in the development of your practice. To investigate wider and more meaningful critical debate and inquiry, you may want to consider becoming actively involved in critical collaborative professional communities that link research to practice. These communities can be developed on the virtual learning environment of your institution or be external. It is important that these critical spaces for professional learning are validated and not seen as 'less than' and 'add ons' to traditional teaching and learning approaches such as lectures and seminars. The idea of professional communities can encourage practitioners towards sharing values. This can offer you the opportunity to share ideas not only on what and how you teach but the very philosophy behind your motivations and the implications of these on your role as a teacher and educator. Professional communities can be with the people you work with, external contacts and members of virtual learning forums such as those located on the excellence gateway (see www.excellencegateway.org.uk/page.aspx?o=usercommunities).

The following case study focuses on Andy, a trainee tutor whose specialism is construction.

Case study: bringing existing skills into teaching

After working on building sites, up and down the country for twenty years, it was a real shock going back into the classroom. I knew I was good at my job, hadn't I been promoted to site manager because of my experience? With management responsibilities my communication and time management skills were also good. But I thought these skills would have nothing to do with my role as a teacher. I almost imagined starting a new career was like starting from scratch, my skills from my previous job, not unlike my trowel being left behind for every teacher' tool – a pen. How wrong I was. The reality is that many of the skills I had used as a brick layer and site manager came to the fore. These included:

- communicating effectively in a team
- organising my own and others' workload
- being on top of my subject specialist knowledge and any new initiatives
- sharing my knowledge
- being punctual and hardworking
- working with different professions. How once I had worked with surveyors, building tradesmen etc., now it was counsellors, mentors, SfL tutors.

Recognising the skills I had developed across my working life allowed me to transfer them to my new role of tutor. Having real experience of my trade is a real asset in maintaining the learners' interest. They value the fact that when I teach it isn't just from a theoretical perspective; I link the theory to practice with anecdotes from my many years of hands on experience. Some of my learners are second generation

---

unemployed and are keen to find out what the world of work is all about and specifically what life's like working for a construction firm. My experience really hooks them in, continues to motivate them and grounds the knowledge in the working lives they plan to pursue.

Getting the most from your teaching

The majority of teaching practitioners in post-compulsory education and training operate within the context of dual professionalism. Having excelled in their vocational or academic specialism in business, industry and commerce, they choose to pass on their skills and expertise to learners in their field. To do this effectively you are or have partaken in teacher training and have been awarded qualifications in recognition of your skills and abilities as a teacher. Keeping on top of your specialist area can give you the confidence to teach in an innovative way.

Balancing home life with work

An important aspect of getting the most out of your teaching is to create a work–life balance now and throughout your career. As with many professions in the public sphere, teaching in the LLS can be very demanding on both your time and your emotions. This can impact on your family life and your health.

The University and College Union (UCU) commissioned a piece of research entitled, *FE Colleges: The Frontline Under Pressure – A Staff Satisfaction Survey of Further Education Colleges in England* (Smith et al., 2008). The research stated that many staff in FE colleges find it difficult to maintain a good work–life balance, are feeling under stress and do not have access to flexible working arrangements to help them manage these pressures. Moreover, this may be being compounded by a sense among some people that they lack job security. Additionally:

- Only 7.4 per cent of respondents do not work beyond their contracted hours.
- Out of the staff who said they often work beyond their contracted hours, 28.9% of teaching staff, 38.2% of managers and 63% of senior managers said they often worked more than 11 additional hours per week.
- 48.3% of people said they are not able to achieve a good work–life balance.
- Just over half of all respondents (53%) say they do not have access to flexible working arrangements.
- Most people (69.8%) say they feel too much stress in their job. Teaching staff are more likely than other groups to say they are stressed, with 73.9% reporting this.
- 45.7% of staff said they do not feel they have job security.

(Villeneuve-Smith et al., 2008: 2–3)

With these findings it is hardly surprising that many of the staff working in FE feel under pressure and are often in states of stress. Often the emotional labour that practitioners invest into their job can be draining (Avis and Bathmaker, 2004). This labour often includes 'underground working' (Gleeson, 2005), such as supporting learners' needs in unaccounted time slots, for example, breaks and lunchtimes. The time, energy and commitment of a working week based on extra hours can often leave staff emotionally exhausted. This may be compounded by work environments where job security is unstable due to redundancies and restructuring, leaving practitioners reluctant to reveal their true emotions in case they are labelled as not coping and sidelined for redundancies.

If the pressure of work is overwhelming, rather than brushing worries under the desk, it is worth speaking to your mentor or/and tutor. Together you can explore strategies to address difficulties, perhaps through appropriate CPD activities (Kennedy, 2005; Orr, 2008).

A culture of working long hours

In an age of global capitalism, most FE establishments are built on a business model where targets and outputs often dictate the working week. As such achieving them can take much longer than average 40-hour working week. Taking work home can eat into our personal time with family/friends. This can lead to friction at home and burn-out, if not addressed.

Commuting

Commuting involves much more than just covering the distance between home and work. Commuting can not only take time, but can also generate out-of-pocket costs, cause stress and impact on the relationship between work and family.

Temporary contracts

In times of economic uncertainty, FE establishments often increase the number of people employed on a temporary basis rather than putting them on permanent contracts. This allows them to chop and change structures much more easily, without the large costs involved with redundancy: instead, they just do not renew temporary contracts.

There are, however, advantages to temporary contracts:

- you can escape the office politics that are a common feature in many organizations
- it is an ideal way to earn some extra cash for a short period of time, such as the run-up to the holidays and Christmas
- it is a perfect option for newly qualified graduates or parents looking to return to work after raising a family
- you can test out different roles without committing to the long term.

There are also disadvantages to temporary contracts:

- irregular work: hard to plan ahead as the number of hours you work one week may be different the next, which will hit your pocket
- temporary workers have very few rights and this can leave you in a difficult situation when it comes to sick leave, maternity and holiday pay.

The following case study focuses on health and social care specialist, Angela Court-Jackson.

Case study: feeling under pressure

As a trainee teacher, one can very easily move from feeling on top of things to feeling like things are piling up on you at an alarming rate. It's easy to become convinced that the demands of a rigorous academic course and, indeed, the lecturers are directly responsible for the tiredness that can come with hard work and even the decline in the quality of one's personal life. Abdicating responsibility is sometimes easier than accepting personal responsibility for when things aren't going as well as they could be.

In 1954, Julian Rotter studied the concept of people's beliefs about who or what was responsible for their bad luck or good fortune, and his work is still used today in a number of areas such as health and educational psychology.

The Locus of Control test is an interesting and effective way of getting people to think about their levels of self efficacy and to consider their current ways of thinking. Essentially, it's a way of assessing how much control you're taking in (and accepting for) your own life. This was a means to helping me take responsibility for my actions.

Also, collecting and reflecting upon feedback from one's peers was an important part of my development. It's not all going to be positive, but that's the point; it steered me, and kept me from ever becoming complacent. Learning the value of feedback that early in my teaching career was truly invaluable for my future development.

Thinking about how we manage our work commitments

Your employers can also look at strategies to support you in striking a balance between home/work life.

They may put into place:

- flexible working arrangements
- leave provision for emergencies
- staff benefits such as employee counselling, gym membership and child care vouchers
- have an open door policy where you can be approached if support is needed.

We all have times when we are especially busy and need to put in extra hours. But, for a healthy work–life balance, that situation needs to be the exception rather than the norm. We work best when our lives are in balance. Ideally, your work should interest you. You should enjoy the contact with your colleagues and essentially the teaching. It should be fulfilling while leaving you time to enjoy the other aspects of your life – your friends and family, your hobbies and other interests. In order to strike a balance you need to work effectively and take the right decision to support this. Work–life balance will be different for each of us and will change over our working and personal lives.

Conclusion

Teamwork is an essential part of being successful in your job. Sharing your own thoughts, skills, knowledge and ideas can also be a way to develop your confidence. The key to effective teamwork is effective communication. Remember your colleagues are there to support the learners, but also you are there to support each other in striving to be the best teacher you can be.

References

Avis, J. and Bathmaker, A.-M. (2004) The politics of care: emotional labour and trainee further education lecturers, *Journal of Vocational Education and Training*, 56(1): 5–20.

Department for Education and Skills (DfES) (2004) *Equipping our Teachers for the Future: Reforming Initial Teacher Training for the Learning and Skills Sector*. London: DfES.

Duckworth, V. and Taylor, K. (2008) Words are for everyone, *Research and Practice in Adult Literacy*, 64: 30–2.

Gleeson, D. (2005) Learning for change in further education, *Journal of Vocational Training and Education*, 57(2): 239–46.

Hyland, T. and Merrill, B. (2003) *The Changing Face of Further Education*. London: RoutledgeFalmer.

Kennedy, A. (2005) Models of continuing professional development: a framework for analysis, *Journal of In-Service Education*, 31(2): 235–50.

Lifelong Learning UK (LLUK) *New Overarching Professional Standards for Teachers, Tutors and Trainers in the Lifelong Learning Sector*. London: LLUK.

Orr, K. (2008) Room for improvement? The impact of compulsory professional development for teachers in England's further education sector, *Journal of In-service Education*, 34(1): 97–108.

Rotter, J.B. (1954) *Social Learning and Clinical Psychology*. New York: Prentice Hall.

Villeneuve-Smith, F., Munoz, S. and McKenzie, E. (2008) *FE Colleges: The Frontline Under Pressure? A Staff Satisfaction Survey of Further Education Colleges in England*. London: Learning and Skills Network.

Further reading

The following books are some suggestions for further reading relating to the themes raised in this book. This is by no means an exhaustive list. Rather, we have aimed to list some of those books/articles that we have drawn on in the past, some of which we have used with our own students and some of which we have written in the past.

Abramson, M., Bird, J. and Stennett, A. (eds) (1996) *Further and Higher Education Partnerships: The Future for Collaboration*. Buckingham: Open University Press/Society for Research into Higher Education.

Armitage, A., Bryant, R., Dunnill, R., Renwick, M., Hayes, D., Hudson, A., Kent, J. and Lawes, S. (2003) *Teaching and Training in Post-compulsory Education*, 2nd edn. Maidenhead: Open University Press.

Avis, J. (2002) Developing staff in further education: discourse, learners and practice, *Research in Post-compulsory Education*, 7(3): 339–52.

Avis, J., Fisher, R. and Thompson, R. (eds) (2010) *Teaching in Lifelong Learning: A Guide to Theory and Practice*. Maidenhead: McGraw Hill/Open University Press.

Ball, S. (2008) *The Education Debate*. Bristol: The Policy Press.

Barton, D., Hamilton, M. and Ivanic, R. (eds) (2000) *Situated Literacies: Reading and Writing in Context*. London: Routledge.

Beck, U. (1992) *Risk Society*. London: Sage Publications.

Carr, W. and Kemmis, S. (1986) *Becoming Critical: Education, Knowledge and Action Research* reprint. London: RoutledgeFalmer.

Crowther, J., Hamilton, M. and Tett, L. (eds) (2001) *Powerful Literacies*. Leicester: National Institute for Adult Continuing Education.

Duckworth, V. and Taylor, K. (2008) Words are for everyone, *Research and Practice in Adult Literacy*, 64: 30–2.

Duckworth, V. (2009) *'Into Work'* 14–19 series. Warrington: Gatehouse Books.

Duckworth, V., Wood, J., Dickinson, J. and Bostock, J. (2010) *Successful Teaching Practice in the Lifelong Learning Sector*. Exeter: Learning Matters.

Eraut, M. (1994) *Developing Professional Knowledge and Competence*. Abingdon: RoutledgeFalmer.

Field, J. (2000) *Lifelong Learning and the New Educational Order*. Stoke-on-Trent: Trentham Books.

Hilborne, J. (1996) Ensuring quality in further and higher education partnerships, in M. Abramson, J. Bird and A. Stennett (eds), *Further and Higher Education Partnerships: the Future for Collaboration*. Buckingham: Open University Press/Society for Research into Higher Education.

Hooks, B. (1984) *Feminist Theory: From Margin to Center*. Boston, MA: South End Press.

Ivanic, R., Edwards, R., Barton, D., Martin-Jones, M., Fowler, Z., Hughes, B., Mannion, G., Miller, K., Satchwell, C. and Smith, J. (2009) *Improving Learning in College: Rethinking Literacies Across the Curriculum*. London: Routledge.

James, D. and Biesta, G. with Colley, H., Davies, J., Gleeson, D., Hodkinson, P., Maull, W., Postlethwaite, K. and Wahlberg, M. (2007) *Improving Learning Cultures in Further Education*. London: Routledge.

Knight, P.T. and Yorke, M. (2003) *Assessment, Learning and Employability*. Maidenhead: Open University Press/Society for Research into Higher Education.

Lea, J., Hayes, D., Armitage, A., Lomas, L. and Markless, S. (2003) *Working in Post-compulsory Education*. Maidenhead: Open University Press.

Lillis, T. (2001) *Student Writing: Access, Regulation, Desire*. London: Routledge.

Mansell, W. (2007) *Education by Numbers: The Tyranny of Testing*. London: Politico's.

Meighan, R. and Harber, C. (2007) *A Sociology of Educating*. London: Continuum.

Osborne, M., Houston, M. and Toman, N. (eds) (2007) *The Pedagogy of Lifelong Learning*. London: Routledge.

Schön, D.A. (1990) *Educating the Reflective Practitioner: Toward a New Design for Teaching and Learning in the Professions*. San Francisco, CA: Jossey-Bass.

Taylor, I. (1997) *Developing Learning in Professional Education*. Buckingham: Open University Press/Society for Research into Higher Education.

Tight, M. (2002) *Key Concepts in Adult Education and Training*, 2nd edn. London: RoutledgeFalmer.

Tummons, J. (2007) *Assessing Learning in the Lifelong Learning Sector*, 2nd edn. Exeter: Learning Matters.

Tummons, J. (2007) *Becoming a Professional Tutor in the Lifelong Learning Sector*. Exeter: Learning Matters.

Tummons, J. (2009) *Curriculum Studies in the Lifelong Learning Sector*. Exeter: Learning Matters.

Wallace, S. (2002) No good surprises: intending lecturers' preconceptions and initial experiences of further education, *British Educational Research Journal*, 28(1): 79–93.

Wenger, E. (1998) *Communities of Practice: Learning, Meaning and Identity*. Cambridge: Cambridge University Press.

Index

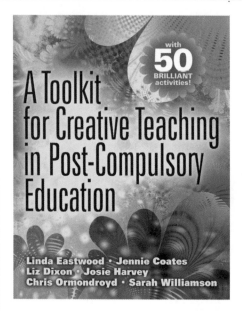

TRANSFORMING FORMATIVE ASSESSMENT IN POST-COMPULSORY EDUCATION

Kathryn Ecclestone with
    Jennie Davies, Jay Derrick
    and Judith Gawn

978-0-335-23654-1 (Paperback)
2010

eBook also available

This unique book combines theory, research and practical insights to demonstrate how teachers' understanding of formative assessment can be enhanced. It aims to improve assessment practices in post-compulsory education (PCE), drawing on well-designed and rigorous research studies.

Coverage includes:

- What impact do political and social factors have on assessment practices?
- Why do similar assessment practices have different effects in different 'learning cultures'?
- How can teachers, lecturers and other education professionals improve formative assessment?

This book is essential reading for teachers, trainee teachers and others working in the lifelong learning sector.

www.openup.co.uk

OPEN UNIVERSITY PRESS
McGraw - Hill Education

Supporting Learners
in the Lifelong Learning Sector

SUPPORTING LEARNERS IN THE LIFELONG LEARNING SECTOR

Marilyn Fairclough

978-0-335-23362-5 (Paperback) 2008

eBook also available

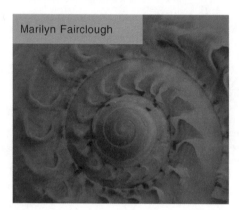

Marilyn Fairclough

This is the first book of its kind to deal with the topic of *supporting* learners in PCET, rather than just focusing on how to teach them.

Key features:

- Each chapter cross-referenced to the QTLS Professional Standard for those on PTLLS, CTLLS and DTLLS courses
- Real life examples from a variety of settings and subjects
- Practical suggestions for developing classroom practice
- Suggestions for managing disruptive behaviour

 **OPEN UNIVERSITY PRESS**
McGraw · Hill Education

www.openup.co.uk